GAME CHANGERS
The Greatest Plays in
Alabama
Football History

Kirk McNair

TRIUMPH
B O O K S

For my wife, Lynne, and my children, Julia and Stuart; for the players and coaches who have made Alabama football special; and for the fans of the Crimson Tide

Library of Congress Cataloging-in-Publication Data

McNair, Kirk, 1945–
  Game changers : the greatest plays in Alabama football history / Kirk McNair.
    p. cm.
  ISBN 978-1-60078-260-2
  1. Alabama Crimson Tide (Football team)—History. 2. University of Alabama—Football—History.
I. Title.
  GV958.A4M37 2009
  796.332'630976184—dc22

                                                              2009015353

This book is available in quantity at special discounts for your group or organization. For further information, contact:
  Triumph Books
  542 South Dearborn Street
  Suite 750
  Chicago, Illinois 60605
  (312) 939-3330
  Fax (312) 663-3557
  www.triumphbooks.com

Printed in China
ISBN: 978-1-60078-260-2
Design by Sue Knopf/Patricia Frey
Page production by Patricia Frey
Photos courtesy of the Paul W. Bryant Museum unless otherwise indicated

Contents

Foreword

I first heard about this project in the midst of a wonderful year for the Alabama football team. A group of people held together by the common denominator of Alabama football had gathered at the home of Ken and Jessie Fowler, as we had done for many years on Tuscaloosa game days. Their spacious home—just a short walk from Bryant-Denny Stadium—could not be better for pre- and postgame exchanges. The Fowler table, overseen by Jessie, is always loaded with sumptuous treats. The talk is always lively and very rarely drifts away from Alabama football. Opinions about what is wrong are followed by ways to correct it; opinions about what is right are followed by ways to keep it that way. Ken, a wonderful, generous host, keeps everyone on his toes with friendly gibes. He is not hesitant to explain in detail how Alabama will dominate that day's opponent. Ken is usually right.

Kirk McNair, whom I have known since the 1960s, and I stood at one of the snack tables. I had chip in hand when Jessie warned, "Be careful. I prepared that dip for Fred and it is hot." Fred Sington Jr., a former Alabama player, is a regular at the Fowlers'. I took a chance and so did Kirk, and then we went in search of cool liquids.

As we regained our breath and composure with iced beverages, Kirk told me he was about to start a new book. That did not surprise me. I suspect no one has written more on Alabama football, including all or parts of several books on the subject. And he has done so with great success. I know of no one more qualified than Kirk McNair to delve into Alabama football history. He has been a vital part of Bama football and sports for many years.

He told me the book would be about the greatest plays in Alabama history. I said, "Wow, that is some undertaking!" During and after my 30-plus years of broadcasting on the Alabama Football Network, I have had scores of people ask, "What was the greatest game you ever broadcast?" I could never come up with an answer. I couldn't select one out of 300-plus games. And now Kirk was going

to pick out the best of the best from literally thousands and thousands of plays. Intriguing.

The more I toyed with the idea, the more I liked it. I remembered something my brother Dale told me when he played for the Crimson Tide. He said that coach Paul Bryant told the team, "All anyone can ask a player to do is concentrate and be focused on the task at hand for a maximum of six to seven seconds at a time." That's the average time it takes to run a play in football. All of us have heard many times that there are four to six plays that will determine the winner of a game; since the players do not know when one of those game-winning plays will occur, for every play, they have to put everything out there for six or seven seconds at a time. If you do, chances are your team will prevail.

So we have, in this book, a compilation of the greatest plays in Alabama history. Of course, there are plays that

happened a very long time ago that certainly have contributed to the great history and mystique that is Alabama football. There are many others you can be assured, but the ones inside these covers are worthy entrants into such a lineup.

Remember how long Coach Bryant said it took to run a play? Six to seven seconds. With that in mind, let us turn the pages and get into the greatest plays in Alabama football history. That amounts to about 259 seconds, something under five minutes, that all Bama fans will surely delight in; a few minutes that made Alabama one of the greatest names in college football. And I'll bet after reading you will come up with a few "seven seconds of history" of your own. Enjoy! And "Roll Tide!"

—Doug Layton

Introduction

Legendary Alabama coach Paul Bryant wasn't the first to say and do everything in football, but much of what I know about the game I learned from the fortunate experience of having worked with him for the final 15 years of his extraordinary career. One thing he said, and something that virtually all other coaches agree on, is that a close game will ordinarily be decided by a handful of big plays. Every game-deciding play is not included within the pages of *Game Changers: The Greatest Plays in Alabama Football History*, and some of the plays that are included were extracted from games that were not close.

Not all of Alabama's games have been close, of course. With a football history dating from 1892, Alabama has played more than 1,150 games. Alabama's remarkable football tradition ranks among the nation's best with 800 wins, 56 bowl game appearances, 31 bowl victories, 12 national championships, 21 Southeastern Conference championships, and 29 10-win seasons. Former

Alabama coach Gene Stallings said football success is about providing opportunities for "players to make plays." More than 100 times Alabama players have made the plays that earned them All-America recognition.

With numerous big plays in Alabama football history from which to choose, our task was to pick out the greatest and most memorable. These plays didn't come to us chiseled on stone tablets. These may not be all of the greatest plays in Alabama history. Huge plays of great importance to Crimson Tide success and Bama tradition date from the 1920s when Dr. George Denny made the decision that football would be important at and to The University of Alabama. Hall of Fame coaches Wallace Wade and Frank Thomas were extraordinarily successful from 1923 through 1946, and under their leadership were many, many great plays.

By any measure, these plays from the distant past are among the greatest in Alabama football history. What we lack in these legendary plays, however, is the means to accurately describe the details. Colorful reports enable us to put them into context as to importance in the season and/or the history and tradition of Alabama football. Therefore, we pay tribute to them here.

Johnny Mack Brown, who would go on to movie fame as a cowboy star, caught passes of 58 yards from Grant Gillis and 62 yards from Pooley Hubert to propel Bama to a 20–19 victory over Washington in Alabama's first Rose Bowl appearance on January 1, 1926. In Bama's 29–13 win over Stanford in the 1934 Rose Bowl, Dixie Howell rushed for 111 yards and completed nine of 13 passes for 160 yards, and Don Hutson caught six passes for 165 yards and scored on passing plays of 59 and 30 yards.

Alabama's first national football headlines came in 1922 when it upset powerful Penn 9–7 in Philadelphia. If Penn beat Alabama today, it would be an upset of similar proportions. The winning play was Alabama's Shorty Propst recovering Hubert's fumble in the end zone.

A case could be made that the greatest play was whatever the first one was, when head coach E.B. Beaumont's 1892 team played a team of Birmingham high school all-stars and won 56–0. The sport—known to few and barely resembling today's game—was under way in Tuscaloosa.

Coach Bryant's favorite play? "When one of our players tosses the ball to the official in the end zone," he said.

For the purpose of accuracy, the plays in this book date from the 1959 season on. Even with this restricted choice, narrowing the plays down was a labor—a labor of love, to be sure, but labor nonetheless. Not every great play could be included.

The longest rush in Alabama history—96 yards by Chris Anderson against Temple in 1991—didn't make the list. Neither did the longest pass—Freddie Kitchens to Michael Vaughn for 94 yards against Florida in the SEC Championship Game in 1996.

The task was not to find enough worthy plays. At Alabama there is an embarrassment of football riches; our first working list included 87 plays. For that reason, we accept that knowledgeable Crimson Tide followers might disagree with our choices. In 1979, Coach Bryant took a call on *Bear Line*, the Monday night radio call-in show hosted by Doug Layton. A caller offered coaching advice, and Bryant replied, "You get yourself a football team together and do it however you want to."

Selection of the 50 plays was less by criteria than by flow chart. A play was great for its effect on the moment. What was the importance beyond that? For example, did the play have a bearing on a national championship, the goal of Alabama teams and the standard by which Bama squads are measured? Finally, did the play reach the level of "great"?

I have been fortunate to see most of these plays in person, primarily as a reporter. I saw a few as a spectator from the stands, including Ken Stabler's "Run in the Mud" against Auburn at the end of the 1967 season. I am comfortable I gave the challenge my best effort. So with noted exceptions, here are the greatest plays in Alabama football history. Perhaps we should add, "So Far." I have no doubt there will be many more.

Creating a Legend

Johnny Musso scored two touchdowns out of the wishbone to lead Bama to an upset victory over USC in the 1971 season opener.

September 10, 1971

Wishbone Unveiled

Decade of Dominance Begins with Offensive Surprise and Upset of USC

Alabama had ended 1970 with the Crimson Tide's second consecutive five-loss season and an appearance in a midlevel bowl game, the Astro-Bluebonnet Bowl. Oklahoma—a team that had switched to the new wishbone offense favored by its rival Texas—and Alabama tied the game 17–17.

Alabama's team airplane left Houston for the return to Tuscaloosa on January 1. Crimson Tide coach Paul Bryant reached into his briefcase and pulled out a yellow legal pad and unclipped a fountain pen from his shirt pocket. Bryant spent the hour in the air sketching out the wishbone ground attack.

Bryant was familiar with the formation because he had just prepared his team to play against it. No one will ever know exactly when he made the decision to switch Alabama to the wishbone.

"We don't awe anyone now," Bryant said before the 1971 season. "We are back among the ordinary folk, and I don't like it."

"He told us in late August," said Mal Moore, an assistant coach who was going to be coaching quarterbacks for the first time at Bama. Moore said Bryant and Texas coach Darryl Royal spent time together during the summer and

that Bryant no doubt quizzed Royal on the offense. "Coach Royal was going to speak at the coaching clinic we had every August during all-star week," Moore said. "Usually the assistant coaches spent a lot of time during the clinic with high school coaches, but this year was different."

Emory Bellard was a member of the Texas coaching staff and the man credited with developing the wishbone. "We had a chalkboard and a projector," Moore said. "We looked at cut-ups [wishbone plays] over and over and over. He coached us like we were students and it was a cram course. It was complicated. We went over footwork and blocking and counting the defense, everything that goes into it."

In the wishbone, Alabama went from two wide receivers to one. The fullback was right behind the quarterback. Slightly behind the fullback and to either side were the halfbacks.

Alabama had used a version of the formation for years. That Bama version of the full-house backfield was grind-it-out power football. The triple-option wishbone was a combination of power, deception, and ball handling.

Bama's opening game in 1971 was a Friday night matchup in the Los Angeles Coliseum against Southern Cal. The Trojans of coach John McKay had beaten Alabama in Birmingham the year before by a score of 42–21, and it was believed the only reason it wasn't worse was that McKay and Bryant were such good friends.

"We went to Los Angeles with a real basic offense," Moore said. "We had only been practicing it a few weeks. But the triple option is a lot of offense, three plays in one."

The wishbone was kept secret. Each August a few dozen reporters boarded an airplane in Birmingham and made the trek to each Southeastern Conference school to watch each team practice and to get comments from coaches and players. The expedition was known as the "SEC Sky-Writers."

"I remember the day the Sky-Writers came in and we wasted a day of practice running the old offense," Tide star running back Johnny Musso said. "It was fun to think we were going to pull it off."

In pregame warm-ups, Moore got a bad feeling. "We kept fumbling the snap," he said. "Everyone was nervous. I was afraid we wouldn't make a first down."

"I was pretty confident in the offense," Musso said. "We had John Hannah and Buddy Brown at guards and Jim Krapf at center. That's the heart of the wishbone and we had three guys who could make All-America. And we had a fantastic quarterback to run the wishbone. I don't think Terry Davis ever got the appreciation he deserved. We had some great wishbone quarterbacks after Terry, but I don't think there was ever anyone better."

On Alabama's first possession, the Tide ran its basic wishbone play: 36. Davis took the snap and moved to his right. Fullback Ellis Beck was running on a line just outside the right tackle. Davis put the ball in Beck's gut, but pulled it back when USC's defensive end stepped toward Beck. Davis continued down the line. When the outside linebacker came toward Davis, he pitched to Musso, who was following the block of right halfback Joe LaBue.

Alabama scored on its first three possessions—two Musso touchdown runs and a Bill Davis field goal. The defense held the Trojans to 10 points for the 17–10 Bama win.

Moore said Alabama threw only six passes on the night. "Five were complete and one was intercepted," he said. The passing yardage was a meager 38 yards, but Alabama had 302 yards rushing and outgained USC in total offense 340–287.

Bryant's change to the wishbone may well have extended his career. From the first game in 1971 until he finished his amazing career in 1982, Bryant's record with the wishbone offense was 124–19–1 and included nine Southeastern Conference championships and three national titles.

Musso said, "I think the wishbone energized Coach Bryant. I think the two previous seasons took a lot out of him. But he said, 'Enough is enough.' He got energized, got a new focus, and quickly turned the program around."

> **W**e had a real fine offensive plan. It was to try to keep the football as much as we could.
>
> —PAUL BRYANT, ALABAMA COACH

Game Details

Alabama 17 • Southern Cal 10

Alabama	10	7	0	0	**17**
Southern Cal	0	10	0	0	**10**

Date: September 10, 1971

Team Records: Alabama 0-0, Southern Cal 0-0

Scoring Plays:

UA Musso 13-yard rush (Davis kick)
UA Davis 37-yard field goal
UA Musso 8-yard rush (Davis kick)
USC Young 7-yard pass from Jones (Rae kick)
USC Rae 37-yard field goal

Mal Moore

Quarterback Mal Moore was recruited in Paul Bryant's first freshman class. He played on Alabama's 1961 national championship team and was an assistant coach for Bama on national championship teams in six other seasons—1964, 1965, 1973, 1978, 1979, and 1992. He was quarterbacks coach and offensive coordinator under Bryant, and then returned to Alabama in 1990 in that capacity under Gene Stallings.

He went to the administrative side in 1994 and in 1999 was appointed Alabama's director of athletics. He has overseen a massive facilities upgrade, including expansions of Bryant-Denny Stadium to over 100,000 seats. The building housing Alabama's athletics administration offices, football offices, weight room, practice locker rooms, training rooms, and media center was named in his honor in 2007.

Mal Moore was an assistant coach on six of Alabama's national championship teams.

December 29, 1982

Last Roundup

Bryant Goes Out a Winner as Sack Preserves Liberty Bowl Victory

Alabama's football history is built in great part on the Crimson Tide's extraordinary bowl success. For as long as anyone can remember, Bama has been the leader in bowl game participation and bowl victories. For many years, a bowl game was a reward for an outstanding season, and there weren't very many bowl games. In recent years a proliferation of bowl games has allowed teams with flawed credentials to enter the postseason arena.

Alabama earned its early reputation because of great success in the Rose Bowl, tantamount to the national championship game in the 1920s and '30s. Alabama has played in its share of less-prestigious bowl games, too. For the most part, the results of those games drift into insignificance. A notable exception is the Liberty Bowl at the conclusion of the 1982 season, a game matching middle-of-the-road teams Alabama and Illinois. In any other year, the game would have

been of little attraction. This year was different. Paul W. Bryant was "a senior."

"Coach Bryant told us he was one of the seniors this year," senior defensive end Mike Pitts said. "It was emotional. For a lot of us, it was our last game. It meant a lot for Coach Bryant to put himself in our position. We knew he would be doing all he could to win this game, and we wanted to do everything we could."

It was no secret that the Liberty Bowl would be the final game for Bryant. He had announced his intentions following the regular season, and his successor, Ray Perkins, already had been introduced. The Liberty Bowl in Memphis was an instant sellout. Requests for press credentials were overwhelming.

The historic aspect of the game was not lost on Alabama players who felt enormous pressure to succeed. Defensive tackle Randy Edwards said, "Before the game, we talked about what it meant, how historic this game was, and how we'd have to live for the rest of our lives and regret it if we got beat."

Alabama's 21–15 victory over Illinois in 1982 marked the 323rd and final win in coach Paul Bryant's career. *Photo courtesy of AP Images*

Paul Bryant

Dozens of books, thousands of articles, and millions of stories chronicled the life of Paul William "Bear" Bryant, considered the greatest college football coach of all time. For a dazzling quarter of a century (1958–82), he was the coach of his alma mater,

Alabama. Even after Gene Stallings coached Alabama to a national championship in 1992, he observed, "Alabama loves Coach Bryant and just tolerates the rest of us." Bryant had a career record of 323–85–17 in 38 years of coaching at Maryland, Kentucky, Texas A&M, and Alabama. His Alabama record was 232–46–9. His Alabama teams won six national championships (1961, '64, '65, '73, '78, '79) and finished in the top 10 another 13 seasons. Bryant's Bama teams won 13 SEC championships. He also won one at Kentucky. He was SEC Coach of the Year 10 times and national Coach of the Year in 1961, 1971, and 1973. The award now bears his name. His Alabama teams won more games than any other team in the nation in the 1960s and again in the 1970s. The Tide went to 24 bowl games in his 25 years (12–10–2). Alabama won all 25 homecoming games under Bryant. His record in Tuscaloosa was 72–2 (including a 57-game winning streak), and in Birmingham (Alabama's other home stadium) it was 68–15–5. He was inducted into the National Football Foundation Hall of Fame in 1983, his first year of eligibility. Alabama's stadium was renamed Bryant-Denny Stadium in 1975. It is on Bryant Drive in Tuscaloosa, which leads to the Paul W. Bryant Museum. Alabama athletes study in the academic center named Bryant Hall. The most outstanding men's and women's scholar-athletes at The University each year receive the Paul W. Bryant Award. Hundreds of students have attended The University on Bryant Scholarships from a fund he established before his death. Former SEC commissioner Dr. Boyd McWhorter once remarked, "When you are with him, you feel you are with history."

Paul Bryant won six national championships during his 25 seasons as the head coach of his alma mater.
Photo courtesy of 'BAMA Magazine

Perhaps because of subfreezing weather, the game was filled with mistakes. There were 14 turnovers, nine by Illinois, which was making its first bowl trip in 19 years.

Illinois was not a pushover. Tony Eason was an outstanding quarterback for the Illini. Alabama's defense would give up 444 yards of total offense and surrender a Liberty Bowl–record 423 yards of passing to Eason, who completed 35 of 55 passes.

Late in the game Alabama was clinging to a 21–15 lead, but the Illini had moved to the Crimson Tide 30.

Bama players said there was a lot of talk in the huddle. "We were telling each other, 'We've got to win; we've got to win,'" said strong safety Tommy Wilcox.

Senior defensive end Russ Wood said, "Every time we'd get into a tough situation, in the huddle someone would say, 'Coach Bryant.' That was the word—Coach Bryant—every time we were in a tough spot."

In this tough spot, Wood was at right end. At the snap of the ball, Wood attacked from the blind side. Eason, scanning downfield for a receiver, never saw Wood. In a hard-hitting game, Wood delivered one of the hardest licks. The sack sent Eason to the sideline.

The Illinois backup quarterback surrendered the seventh and final interception of the night to linebacker Robbie Jones. Alabama had won Paul Bryant's final game. That was far better than the loss Bryant's first Alabama bowl team had suffered in 1959, ironically in the Liberty Bowl, which was then played in Philadelphia.

Cornerback and game MVP Jeremiah Castille said, "It was very important to win this game. Coach Bryant has done so much for football, and so much for The University. For us, going out and winning this game is saying, 'This is what we can do for you.' There is no way that we can repay him for all he's done. He's been a champion all his life, and it was our job to make sure he went out a champion."

Mike White, head coach of the Illini, said, "Alabama is so quick, so fast, that we were unable to run the ball with any kind of effectiveness. It put a lot of pressure on Tony to read the coverage and make key decisions. It ended up being the game we didn't want to play."

Game Details

Alabama 21 • Illinois 15

Alabama	7	0	7	7	**21**
Illinois	0	6	0	9	**15**

Date: December 29, 1982
Team Records: Alabama 7–4, Illinois 7–4
Scoring Plays:

UA Moore 4-yard rush (Kim kick)
UI Curtis 1-yard rush (kick failed)
UA Bendross 8-yard rush (Kim kick)
UI Williams 2-yard pass from Eason (pass failed)
UI Bass 23-yard field goal
UA Turner 1-yard rush (Kim kick)

The final wishbone game in Bama history provided 217 bruising yards. Fullback Ricky Moore led Bama in rushing with 13 carries for 65 yards. Walter Lewis hit on seven of 13 passes for 130 yards. He found Jesse Bendross three times for 51 yards and Joey Jones twice for 60 yards. Moore, Bendross, and fullback Craig Turner scored Bama touchdowns.

Back in his office on January 3, 1983, five days after the Liberty Bowl, Bryant said, "It was my last roundup. Winning will make my future much more enjoyable." On January 26, four weeks after his final coaching victory, Paul William "Bear" Bryant died of a heart attack at the age of 69.

> **W**hether the team likes it or not, they will always be remembered for winning my last game. I'm proud they wanted to win this one for me.
>
> **—PAUL BRYANT, ALABAMA COACH**

November 14, 1981

Goal-Line Stand II

Defensive Stop on Seventh-and-Goal Highlights Bryant's Record-Tying Win

Alabama coach Paul Bryant was accustomed to catcalls from opposing fans following Crimson Tide football games. As he walked off the field in Happy Valley, a Penn State fan yelled, "Hey, Bear! How do we make a yard on you?" The slightest of smiles was visible on Bryant's face.

The Nittany Lions didn't need terribly long memories to recall Alabama's goal-line stand in the Sugar Bowl at the end of the 1978 season. That Crimson Tide effort preserved a Bama victory and elevated No. 2 Alabama over No. 1 Penn State for the national championship.

In 1981, Alabama and Penn State were solid top-10 teams, though not in the national championship picture. As was often the case, the attention was squarely on Bryant.

For years, Alabama opponents had told prospects that Bryant would probably retire soon, hoping to steer top players away from Alabama. Prior to the 1978 season, Charley Thornton, a key advisor to Bryant, suggested Bryant end the rumors by announcing a quest to break Amos Alonzo Stagg's record for most career wins. At the time Bryant was 40 wins shy of Stagg's mark.

In a preseason speech to the Monday Morning Quarterback Club in Birmingham, Bryant surprised everyone when he announced, "If anybody's going to break the record, it might as well be me." He had no plans to retire, he emphasized. He also said he thought he could do it in four years, which would be averaging more than 10 wins per season.

Bryant won 33 games in the first three years of his quest. He began the 1981 season needing eight to tie and nine to break the record.

The opportunity for 314 came at State College, and Bryant's team delivered a 31–16 victory. Obviously Bama had offense, but defensive plays were memorable. The most memorable came on Down Seven.

College football has had its share of fifth downs. Owing to a blunder by officials in 1990, Colorado was awarded a fifth down against Missouri and scored a touchdown on the final play of the game. That win enabled Colorado to go on to the national championship.

Penn State getting seven downs was also due in part to an officiating error, according to no less an authority than Penn State coach Joe Paterno.

Alabama had taken a 24–3 lead at halftime. The Tide kicked off to Penn State to start the second half and the Lions drove to a first down at the Alabama 4-yard line.

Penn State's excellent tailback, Curt Warner, carried twice for two yards to the 2. On third down, Penn State quarterback Todd Blackledge threw a pass into the left corner of the end zone on what was intended to be a fade route. The Penn State receiver slipped and fell, and the pass fell incomplete. Shockingly, an official's flag fell at the feet of Bama cornerback Benny Perrin. Pass interference had been called. (In the postgame press meeting, Paterno admitted, "That wasn't pass interference.")

Now Penn State had first-and-goal at the Alabama 1-yard line. The Tide's goal-line defensive line included Mike Pitts and Russ Wood at ends, Jackie Cline and Randy Edwards at tackles, and Warren Lyles at nose guard. Penn State ran four plays at the middle of the line, handoffs to fullback Mike Meade, then Warner, Meade again, and finally Warner again.

The net total was minus-1. The defense had held, a tremendous boost for Bama and a devastating blow to Penn State's hopes.

Lyles led the jubilant defenders back to the sideline, turning a celebratory somersault. Bryant stepped onto the field to greet his troops with a bow and a tip of his houndstooth hat.

The seven-down stand by the Alabama defense was extraordinary, but there were a couple of other nice defensive sequences. In the second quarter, Bama lost a fumble at its 5-yard line. Two Penn State plays lost two yards and then Wood sacked

The Tide's victory over Penn State in 1981 was Paul Bryant's 314th as head coach, tying him for the most wins in college football history. *Photo courtesy of AP Images*

Warren Lyles

Warren Lyles was an All–Southeastern Conference nose guard. He was named the Defensive Player of the Game in Alabama's 1981 Cotton Bowl victory over Baylor as he made eight tackles, five of them behind the line of scrimmage. Lyles did not get to play in Alabama's Sugar Bowl win over Penn State for the 1978 national championship, but he was a primary defender in the Tide's Sugar Bowl win over Arkansas for the 1979 title. He was a captain of the 1981 Crimson Tide. He had 61 tackles and led the team with four fumble recoveries in 1980 and though injured part of his senior season had 50 tackles and 11 sacks. For his career he made 187 tackles and had 29 sacks. He was drafted by San Diego in the 1982 NFL Draft.

Warren Lyles collected 29 sacks during his Alabama playing career. *Photo courtesy of Barry Fikes*

Blackledge at the 18, forcing a field goal. Late in the game, Penn State was again in the red zone. On a fourth-down pass to the Bama 10-yard line, Perrin stripped the ball away. Penn State had 15 plays inside the Alabama 20 and netted just three points.

"We thought about the 314 wins during the week, but we knew the record would take care of itself eventually," Wood said. "What we were concerned about was getting back into the national championship picture."

In the locker room after the game, Lyles presented the game ball to his coach. Afterward he said, "I feel like a man who had been poor all his life, and suddenly found a million dollars. Make that two million."

Bryant addressed the record before the season began: "A great coach once told me, 'Paul, what you ought to do is get right up there close, and then quit coaching.' I don't want to break Coach Stagg's record, but I don't want to quit coaching, or winning.

"When you talk about the home-run king, people think of Babe Ruth, but it's not Babe Ruth. It's Henry Aaron. Let Stagg be Babe Ruth."

Game Details

Alabama 31 • Penn State 16

Alabama	7	17	0	7	**31**
Penn State	0	3	0	13	**16**

Date: November 14, 1981
Team Records: Alabama 7–1–1, Penn State 7–1
Scoring Plays:

UA Bendross 37-yard pass from Lewis (Trodd kick)
PSU Franco 35-yard field goal
UA Carruth 2-yard rush (Trodd kick)
UA Trodd 27-yard field goal
UA Bendross 3-yard pass from Lewis (Trodd kick)
PSU Williams 41-yard rush (Franco kick)
UA Carter 1-yard rush (Trodd kick)
PSU Robinson 14-yard pass from Rocco (pass failed)

The goal-line stand was great, but being part of 314 is better than that. It's the greatest thing that ever happened to me. You know how great this day is? I can't tell you, because my vocabulary doesn't contain the words.

—WARREN LYLES, ALABAMA NOSE GUARD

Walter Lewis

Walter Lewis quarterbacked Paul Bryant's final football game in 1982 and was a pallbearer for his coach just over a month later. Lewis was a unanimous All–Southeastern Conference quarterback in 1983 and was Most Valuable Player in the Sun Bowl win over SMU. He was 1983 team captain. Although he split playing time at quarterback for three years, he was Bama's starting quarterback as a senior under coach Ray Perkins. In the win over Penn State, Lewis had 205 yards of total offense, 167 yards passing and 38 rushing. As a senior Lewis completed 144 of 256 passes for 1,991 yards and 14 touchdowns and rushed for 338 yards and five touchdowns. Lewis coached at Alabama briefly, then put his engineering degree to work in the business world.

November 28, 1959

Scooter

Alabama Ended Losing Streak to Auburn in Bryant's Second Season

Red Drew's final Tide team in 1954 had been beaten by Auburn. J.B. Whitworth spent three seasons at the helm of Alabama, and each year The Tide lost to the Tigers by convincing scores, including 40–0 in 1957. Paul Bryant had scared the defending national champion Tigers in 1958, but nonetheless lost 14–8 in Bryant's first season as Crimson Tide coach.

In 1959, a simple signal finally ended a five-game losing streak to Bama's rivals from Auburn.

In the fourth quarter at Legion Field, Alabama had a 3–0 lead. "Tommy Brooker had kicked a field goal and with our defense we felt pretty good," quarterback Bobby Skelton said. "But we knew we were just one mistake away from letting it get away. And Auburn was a very good football team.

"We got a little drive going in the fourth quarter."

One of the smallest players on the team was Marlin "Scooter" Dyess, a 5'6" running back who tipped the scales at 148 pounds. Even for Bryant, who bragged about using small, quick players, Dyess was small. He was also Alabama's fastest player, having clocked a 9.8 in the 100-yard dash.

Against Auburn, Dyess was not at his running back position. He was moved to wide receiver.

"Phil Cutchin coached the quarterbacks," Skelton said. "No one had a title like 'offensive coordinator,' but I think he came up with the play."

Skelton said, "The play was an 'automatic.' That meant, no matter what play had been called, in certain situations the automatic would override it. In this case, it depended on where the cornerback was playing. The cornerback had to be worried about Scooter's speed, so I'd check to see where he was playing.

"We came out with Scooter split out seven yards to the right. I saw the cornerback was playing well off him, really deep. The signal was that I'd look at him and grab my facemask, like I was adjusting my helmet. Scooter would then grab his face mask so I'd know he got it."

The signal was simple. Planning the play had not been.

Bryant first toyed with the idea of using Dyess at end prior to the Vanderbilt game, the third game of the season. He decided to wait, not even mentioning it to his coaching staff until the Monday before the Auburn game.

Bryant said, "We realized in spring drills that we weren't a real fast ballclub. Everyone figured it would be up to little ol' Marlin to take off and run away every once in a while if we were going to get that offense going. He runs like a deer and he's so small you can hardly get your arms around him to get him down."

Skelton said, "It was just a little post pattern with Scooter breaking inside. I hit him quickly and he took a couple of steps forward, then broke it outside. And I lost him.

"There were so many people on the sidelines and Scooter was so small, that I didn't know where he was. And then I could tell from the reaction on our bench and in the stands that he had scored.

"That was a big play for Scooter and a big play for me and a big play for Alabama. We started a nice little run on Auburn that day."

Skelton passed only three times that day and completed only one—the touchdown to Dyess.

Marlin "Scooter" Dyess scored the game's only touchdown in Alabama's 10–0 victory over Auburn in 1959, snapping the Tigers' five-game winning streak against the Tide.

Marlin Dyess

Marlin "Scooter" Dyess was a 5'6", 148-pound halfback on Paul Bryant's first two Alabama football teams. Dyess did not participate in spring training prior to his senior season, instead concentrating on running the 100- and 220-yard dashes for the Tide track team. He missed the first half of the 1959 football season with injuries. As a senior, Dyess had only 28 rushes for 121 yards. He caught 10 passes for 149 yards. Dyess carried five times for 24 yards and caught two passes for 45 yards to total 69 yards of offense against Auburn. Dyess won the MVP award for Alabama against Auburn. He was one of the permanent captains (along with Jim Blevins) of the 1959 team.

Marlin Dyess ran for the Tide's track team and was also a captain of the 1959 football team.

Auburn coach Ralph Jordan said, "I couldn't tell much about individuals in Alabama's line because they ganged up so much, but Pat Trammell and Billy Richardson were outstanding in their backfield. And of course, little Dyess hurt us again."

Jordan was not surprised that Bama had a surprise. Before the game he said, "We can expect them to shoot the works. Joel Eaves, who has done our scouting job, tells me that every game Alabama has brought out something new. They're versatile. We've got to be prepared for almost anything."

The 10–0 Alabama win started a four-year Crimson Tide winning streak in which Bama would outscore Auburn 85–0.

Alabama had hoped for a Gator Bowl bid following the win, but no call came from Jacksonville. Bama turned down a chance to play Kentucky in Louisville's Bluegrass Bowl and accepted a bid to meet Penn State in the inaugural Liberty Bowl, then played in Philadelphia. It would start a run of 24 straight Alabama bowl games under Bryant.

The kids were terrific. I couldn't single out any who were more outstanding than the others, but I'll say this: we couldn't have won it without Dyess. He was the greatest end I ever had today.

—PAUL BRYANT, ALABAMA COACH

Game Details

Alabama 10 • Auburn 0

Alabama	0	3	0	7	**10**
Auburn	0	0	0	0	**0**

Date: November 28, 1959
Team Records: Alabama 6–1–2, Auburn 7–2
Scoring Plays:
UA Brooker 27-yard field goal
UA Dyess 39-yard pass from Skelton (Brooker kick)

Bobby Skelton

Bobby Skelton was redshirted in 1958 and split quarterback duties with Pat Trammell in 1959 and 1960. He was also a Tide baseball player who declined a Senior Bowl invitation because he didn't want to lose baseball eligibility. Following his Bama football career, he was named Most Valuable Player in the North-South Shrine Game in Miami. Although he signed a contract with the Denver Broncos, Skelton would make it into the NFL as an official. He was a high school coach and then became an SEC official in 1972 and he worked national championship Orange Bowl games in 1984 and 1985. In 1985 he became an NFL official and worked 13 divisional and conference championship games and Super Bowl XXIII. He was instrumental in implementation of the replay system in the NFL and became a replay official after retirement from on-the-field officiating. Skelton served as commissioner of the Alabama Community College system from 1998 to 2002.

Linnie Patrick scored the clinching fourth-quarter touchdown in Paul Bryant's record-breaking 315th career victory.

November 28, 1981

Run, Linnie, Run

Linnie Patrick Runs Paul Bryant into Record Book

Alabama coach Paul Bryant sometimes would relax in the off-season with a visit to the gaming tables of Las Vegas. Following the 1981 season, Bryant was there with friends, including Larry Lacewell, an assistant coach at Oklahoma. Lacewell, like Bryant, hailed from Fordyce, Arkansas, and had become close to the legendary Crimson Tide coach.

The 1981 season had been historic—Alabama defeated Auburn 28–17 for Bryant's 315th head-coaching victory. That made Bryant No. 1 all-time in college football history.

Oklahoma had an explosive wishbone offense at the time, somewhat different from Bama's wishbone. The Sooners relied on speed, Bama on precise execution.

Lacewell told Bryant he had watched the Tide's season-ending win over Auburn on television. "The only back you have that could play for us is that No. 25," Lacewell said. He was referring to Crimson Tide sophomore halfback Linnie Patrick.

Bryant agreed that Patrick had talent, but admitted "I worry about him fumbling."

Lacewell said, "At Oklahoma, we don't even practice punting. We know we're either going to score or we're going to fumble."

That might work at Oklahoma, but it was intolerable to Bryant.

Linnie Patrick was a high school legend at Walker High School in Jasper, just north of Tuscaloosa. Patrick had been recruited by colleges from coast to coast. When Patrick made his recruiting trip to Alabama, he expected to be fawned over as he had been everywhere else. When he went into Bryant's office, the first thing he heard from the legendary coach was, "Linnie, I've heard a lot about you." Patrick swelled with pride.

Bryant continued, "Most of what I've heard about you is bad. When I was your age, most of what anyone would have heard about me was bad. I came to The University of Alabama and was able to make something of myself. If you'll come here, I'll give you the chance to make something of yourself."

Alabama assistant coaches were aghast at Bryant's tactic, but Patrick took the challenge and signed with the Crimson Tide prior to the 1980 season.

Even though he was Alabama's second-leading rusher (behind fullback Ricky Moore) and averaged 5.5 yards per carry as a sophomore, Patrick was not a starter at left halfback. He played behind Paul Ott Carruth.

Linnie Patrick

Linnie Patrick had been a two-time All-American in high school. In part because of physical problems during his 1980–83 Alabama football career, Patrick fell short of fans' high expectations. Nevertheless, he had a productive Crimson Tide career. Patrick was a four-year letterman as a backup halfback, the first three in Paul Bryant's wishbone, his senior year for head coach Ray Perkins in the I formation. His final season was his best. He rushed 85 times for 454 yards (5.3 yards per rush) with four touchdowns and caught six passes for 58 yards. For his career he rushed 265 times for 1,503 yards (5.5 yards per rush) with 16 touchdowns and had 11 pass receptions for 91 yards. Those numbers paled in comparison to his Walker High School career in which he had 5,045 yards and 47 touchdowns and was ranked second only to Georgia's Herschel Walker among national running back prospects.

Nevertheless, Patrick got the call as Alabama was clinging to a 21–17 lead in the fourth quarter against Auburn at Legion Field in Birmingham. Walter Lewis was at quarterback for the Tide. He was the third of three quarterbacks who would operate the wishbone that day.

Game Details

Alabama 28 • Auburn 17

Alabama	7	0	7	14	**28**
Auburn	0	7	7	3	**17**

Date: November 28, 1981

Team Records: Alabama 8–1–1, Auburn 5–5

Scoring Plays:

UA Gray 1-yard rush (Kim kick)

AU Peoples 63-yard rush (Del Greco kick)

UA Bendross 26-yard pass from Coley (Kim kick)

AU James 2-yard rush (Del Greco kick)

AU Del Greco 19-yard field goal

UA Bendross 38-yard pass from Lewis (Kim kick)

UA Patrick 15-yard rush (Kim kick)

Offensive coordinator Mal Moore did not call a triple-option play from the Auburn 47. It was strictly a power play, left guard Mike Adcock and left tackle Joe Beazley pulling to run interference around right end. Fullback Ricky Moore, who had 25 blocks in the game—10 of them knockdowns—went downfield. Right halfback Jeff Fagan took out Auburn's strong-side linebacker. Lewis made the pitch to Patrick, who turned upfield behind Moore.

Six times Patrick was hit. He maintained his balance, kept pushing forward, and only after three Tigers reached him at the 15 did Patrick go down.

ABC was televising the historic game. Frank Broyles, the longtime Arkansas coach and color man on ABC, exclaimed, "I suspect that's the best run that young man has ever made."

Mal Moore called Alabama plays, sending them into the quarterback by way of a substitute, usually the wide receiver. A few decades earlier, quarterbacks had to call the plays without benefit of coaching help. Green Bay Packers legendary quarterback Bart Starr—who played at Bama in the 1950s—was known to follow a successful play with the same call. Moore took a page from the Starr book. Following Patrick's 32-yard run to the 15, the Tide called another sweep right. Alabama blocking took care of most Auburn defenders and Patrick was barely brushed as he dashed in for the clinching touchdown.

In anticipation of the Alabama victory, a telephone had been installed in Alabama's locker room. That locker room was a boisterous one, with coaches, players, and staff jubilant in celebration. After a short time, the din was quieted. The telephone was ringing. Bryant took the receiver and after a moment said, "Hello, Gipper."

The president of the United States was on the line to congratulate Bryant on breaking Amos Alonzo Stagg's longtime college football coaching record of 314 wins.

> The game is over. The man has made history—315 wins. The basic credo of Paul Bryant is this: "If you believe in yourself, and have dedication and pride and never quit, you will be a winner. The price of victory is high, but so are the rewards."
>
> —KEITH JACKSON, ABC BROADCASTER

Ronald Reagan and Bryant had a history; when Bryant was an Alabama player at the Rose Bowl, he was interviewed by Reagan, then a young radio reporter. Before politics, Reagan would go on to acting success in Hollywood, including his role as famed Notre Dame football player George Gipp, that included the famous line "Win one for the Gipper."

Reagan said, "It is a record all Americans can take pride in. I congratulate you and your team on a great accomplishment."

A few minutes later, Bryant received another congratulatory telephone call, this one from former president Jimmy Carter.

Asked about not being carried off the field by his players, Bryant said, "I ought to be carrying them off, and I would if I was strong enough. I'd take them off one at a time if it took until midnight."

Paul Bryant spoke with President Reagan after passing Amos Alonzo Stagg on college football's all-time career victories list.

January 2, 1978

Making Sure Bear Is Best

Sugar Bowl Matched Two Winningest Coaches

The 1978 Sugar Bowl was all about the head coaches. Paul Bryant had 272 college football coaching victories, more than any other man in the game. Ohio State coach Woody Hayes was next in line with 231.

Almost every moment leading up to the game in New Orleans centered on "Bear vs. Woody," with both coaches lavishing praise on the other. Alabama had a couple of advantages. Ohio State had lost its last regular-season game to its top rival, Michigan, and had no national motivation for a championship. Additionally, the Buckeyes had been in New Orleans for a couple of weeks, getting away from bad weather to prepare for the game; Alabama did all its preparation in Tuscaloosa. There were reports that Ohio State players enjoyed the New Orleans nightlife prior to the game.

A case can be made that the 1977 Alabama team was the finest ever. That squad went through a nonconference schedule that included Nebraska, No. 1 Southern Cal, Louisville, and Miami. Bama would finish the season with an 11–1 record. The Tide had a star-studded cast of players, including future All-America players Ozzie Newsome,

Jim Bunch, Dwight Stephenson, Don McNeal, E.J. Junior, Marty Lyons, and Barry Krauss.

Alabama's wishbone was a finesse offense to the extent that it relied on eliminating a defender without a block. But it was also a physical offense that relied on tough blocking at the point of attack and its halfbacks and the wide receiver being capable of taking out a nimble defender in the open field. And when it was near a goal line, Alabama never shied away from using its muscle.

On its second possession, the Tide overcame a handful of mistakes to make its way to the Ohio State 1-yard line as the first quarter ended. From there it was power, a fourth-down give to Tony Nathan for the touchdown.

Later in the half, Alabama showed something new. Bruce Bolton, a wide receiver, was at the left halfback spot.

Moments before the snap, Bryant asked quarterbacks coach Mal Moore, "What have you got?" Moore told him Bama was running the new play, Bolton at halfback, motion, pass.

"He wasn't happy," Moore said. "Coach Bryant thought that in a tough game if we got inside the 40, we probably

Tony Nathan scored from the 1-yard line to give Alabama an early lead against Woody Hayes' Buckeyes in the 1978 Sugar Bowl.

Jeff Rutledge

Jeff Rutledge was a four-year letterman (1975–78) and three-year starter at quarterback. He passed for 30 touchdowns, breaking Joe Namath's Bama record of 28, and tied Namath and Harry Gilmer with 13 in a season. He completed 207 of 372 passes (55.6 percent) for 3,351 yards and led Alabama to a 33–5 record. He had an Alabama-record 100 consecutive passes without an interception. Rutledge won Super Bowl rings playing for the Los Angeles Rams, New York Giants, and Washington Redskins in his 13-year NFL playing career, and was quarterbacks coach for Arizona in another Super Bowl.

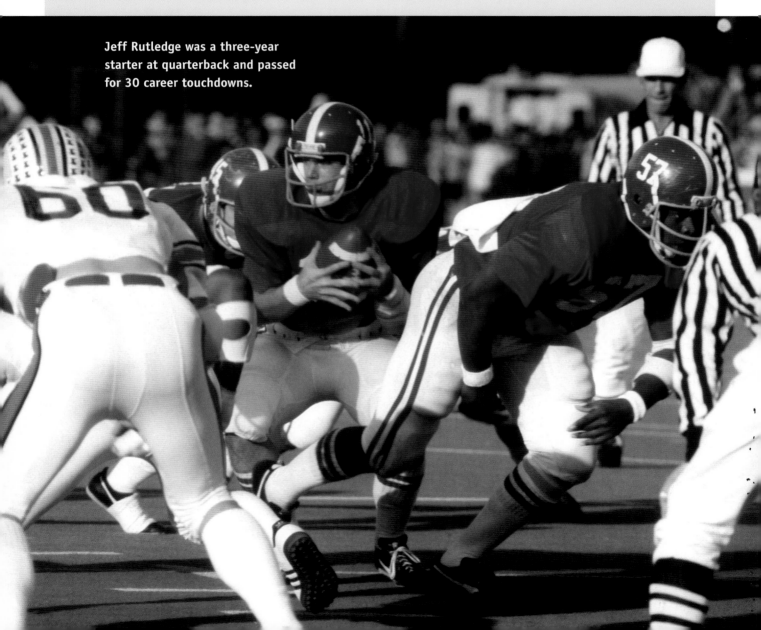

Jeff Rutledge was a three-year starter at quarterback and passed for 30 career touchdowns.

shouldn't pass, that we could get the first down with four runs."

Bolton went in motion to the right, then down the right sideline as quarterback Jeff Rutledge let one fly.

"Everyone on the sideline between me and the goal line stepped out to watch and I couldn't see," Moore said. "Then above the crowd I saw the referee's hands go up. Touchdown."

When Don McNeal and Ricky Tucker stopped Ohio State on fourth down inside the 5-yard line just before intermission, Alabama had a 13–0 halftime lead.

It was still a struggle when Alabama got the ball in the second half. A series of tough wishbone plays got Bama to the Ohio State 3-yard line. The Buckeyes and everyone else in the Louisiana Superdome expected tough running.

Rutledge crossed them up. Alabama's tight end Rick Neal had been Rutledge's high school teammate. Neal lined up on the left side and Rutledge started the wishbone action to the left, faking the handoff to fullback Johnny Davis. Davis always attracted a crowd of defenders. No one paid attention to Neal, who stepped into an open spot in the end zone. Rutledge, a right-handed passer running to his left, had no trouble making the soft pass to Neal for the touchdown. Rutledge completed a two-point conversion pass to Nathan to make it 21–0 and assure that in the battle of Bear vs. Woody, Bama's Bryant would come out on top.

"The pass was always the element of surprise in the wishbone," Rutledge said. "We really didn't want to pass, but when we did, it was often to a receiver who was wide open."

Playing only the first three quarters, Rutledge threw for 109 yards and two touchdowns on 8-of-11 passing. He was an easy winner of the Miller-Digby Award as Sugar Bowl MVP.

Rutledge wasn't nervous during the game. He had been nervous prior to the game, though. "I was a junior with a year of eligibility remaining, but I wanted to get married," he said. "My brother, Gary, had gotten married after his junior season. He told me the toughest thing was going to be getting permission from Coach Bryant. I went to see him while we were practicing for the bowl game and told him Laura and I planned to get married the Saturday after the game.

"He said, 'Do you realize we're getting ready to play Woody Hayes? I've never played against the SOB and now my quarterback wants to get married?'

"But he didn't say I couldn't get married. After the game he said, 'Pretty nice wedding present, huh?'"

> **I** don't think that this game had anything to do with how good a coach I am or how good a coach Woody is. It was just one more game. He's a great coach; and I ain't bad.
>
> —PAUL BRYANT, ALABAMA COACH

Game Details

Alabama 35 • Ohio State 6

Alabama	0	13	8	14	**35**
Ohio State	0	0	0	6	**6**

Date: January 2, 1978

Team Records: Alabama 10–1, Ohio State 9–2

Scoring Plays:

UA Nathan 1-yard rush (Chapman kick)

UA Bolton 27-yard pass from Rutledge (kick failed)

UA Neal 3-yard pass from Rutledge (Nathan pass from Rutledge)

OSU Harrell 38-yard pass from Gerald (pass failed)

UA Ogilvie 1-yard rush (Chapman kick)

UA Davis 7-yard rush (Chapman kick)

Coming Through When It Mattered Most

January 1, 1979

The Goal-Line Stand

With National Championship at Stake, Tide Defense Stopped Penn State

Paul Bryant could not will a national championship, though it sometimes seemed otherwise. Six of the legendary coach's 25 Alabama teams won the title, making national championships the standard for the Crimson Tide. The 1978 team met that measure and contributed a goal-line stand that represents excellence—Bryant's and Alabama's—more than any other on-the-field event in Bama football history.

Late in the 1978 season, Alabama had an outside chance at winning the national championship, but would need a few improbable breaks to earn a bowl matchup against No. 1 Penn State, an independent with no bowl tie-in.

Missouri had to upset Nebraska in Lincoln, or Penn State would be playing Nebraska in the Orange Bowl. Auburn would have to beat Georgia, or the Bulldogs would be going to the Sugar Bowl under an unusual arrangement the Southeastern Conference had with the bowl: in the event two teams tied for the SEC title, and the teams had not played each other, the bowl would invite the team that had been less recently. That would be

Georgia. Improbably, the Tigers did upset the Huskers, and while Auburn didn't beat Georgia, the teams tied, and that was good enough.

Alabama was 10–1 following a difficult schedule. In addition to the rugged SEC slate, Bama's out-of-conference games had been against Nebraska, Missouri, Southern Cal, Washington, and Virginia Tech. Henry Bodenheimer of the Sugar Bowl didn't mince words. "We want an Alabama–Penn State matchup," he said.

And so it was: the first match of No. 1 vs. No. 2 since second-ranked Alabama had been clobbered by national champion Nebraska in the Orange Bowl at the conclusion of the 1971 season. Despite gaudy credentials, Joe Paterno's Penn State team was looking for its first national championship.

The 45th Sugar Bowl was a game in which it seemed the outcome might turn on every play. Tension was as high as it gets. Just a handful of plays made the difference.

Alabama was content to run out the clock with just 1:11 to play in the first half of a scoreless game, but Penn State twice called timeout hoping to get the ball back. The gamble backfired; Bama halfback Tony Nathan ripped off runs of 30 and 7 yards to the Penn State 30. Jeff Rutledge

then completed a pass to Bruce Bolton in the end zone with only eight seconds left on the clock.

In the third quarter, Pete Harris picked off a Rutledge pass, and the Lions took advantage. Chuck Fusina passed to Penn State's fine wide receiver, Scott Fitzkee, deep in the end zone to tie the game 7–7. Minutes later, Lou Ikner returned a Penn State punt 62 yards to the Lions 11-yard line. Three plays later, Major Ogilvie scored from eight yards out to put the Tide up 14–7.

With just under eight minutes to play, Alabama fumbled away a pitchout and Penn State was set up at the Alabama 19. The Lions moved to a first down inside the 10. A rush got nothing, then Fusina hit Fitzkee near the end zone.

"I was covering someone else, but I saw the pass was going to Fitzkee and broke on the ball," said Don McNeal. "I didn't have time to think. It was just instinct. I knew I

Defensively, we played over our heads, just played superhuman football. That goal-line stand was something I'll never forget. I think they are champions. I wanted them to put every ounce of energy into it, and I think they did.

—PAUL BRYANT, ALABAMA COACH

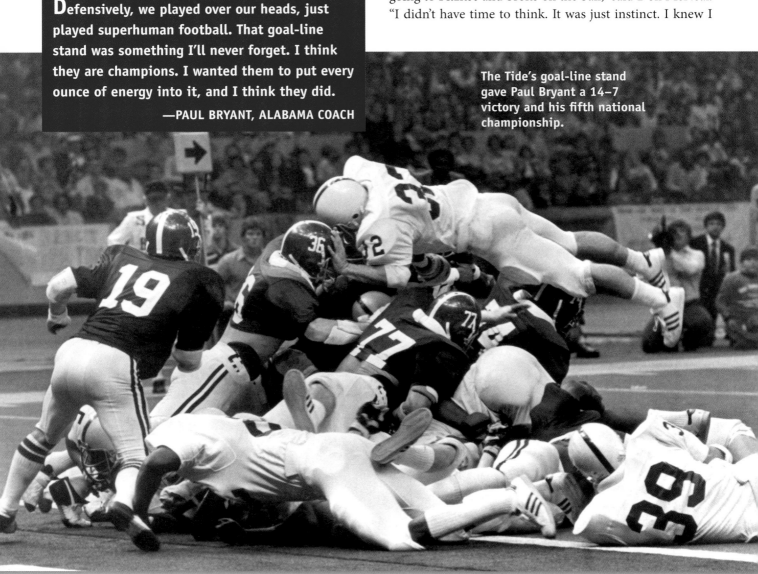

The Tide's goal-line stand gave Paul Bryant a 14–7 victory and his fifth national championship.

had to make a perfect tackle or Fitzkee would fall into the end zone."

On third-and-goal at the 1, Penn State back Matt Suhey was slammed down inside the 1-yard line.

Fusina called timeout to talk to Paterno. When he returned to the line of scrimmage he noticed Tide tackle Marty Lyons standing over the ball.

"How far have we got?" Fusina asked Lyons.

"About 10 inches," Lyons replied. "You'd better pass."

Penn State didn't pass. Instead, running back Mike Guman got the call up the middle.

Linebacker Barry Krauss said, "We had just stopped a dive play, and I thought they would probably play-action or sweep. But Coach Donahue [Bama defensive coordinator Ken Donahue] made a great call for us to play against the inside run again. The defensive line did an incredible job of pushing the Penn State line back.

"So, yes, Guman went over the top, and I was the one who hit him. But that was because of what the defensive line had done. It was Coach Bryant's plan that the defensive line would take out the interference and let the linebackers make the play. And then Murray [Legg] came in and pushed us back, keeping the back from twisting and maybe falling into the end zone. Everyone was involved. It was the epitome of Alabama defense, which was teamwork at its best."

Alabama held on the rest of the way for the 14–7 victory.

Bryant said, "It was the finest defensive effort I can recall. It was the most critical series I can remember."

Game Details

Alabama 14 • Penn State 7

Penn State	0	0	7	0	**7**
Alabama	0	7	7	0	**14**

Date: January 1, 1979
Team Records: Alabama 10–1, Penn State 11–0
Scoring Plays:
UA Bolton 30-yard pass from Rutledge (McElroy kick)
PSU Fitzkee 17-yard pass from Fusina (Bahr kick)
UA Ogilvie 8-yard rush (McElroy kick)

Alabama was a solid No. 1 in the Associated Press voting and in selections by the Football Writers Association of American for the MacArthur Bowl and by the National Football Foundation. Almost inexplicably—particularly since Southern Cal's Rose Bowl win had come via an official's obvious error—the United Press International vote of coaches had USC No. 1 and Bama No. 2. (The two had an equal number of first-place votes, but the Trojans had more second-place votes.)

"That's the first time I can remember that the writers were much more knowledgeable than the coaches," Bryant said.

Barry Krauss

Barry Krauss was an All-American in 1978 and won the Miller-Digby Award as the Most Valuable Player in the Sugar Bowl. Two years earlier he had been MVP of the Liberty Bowl for his play in Alabama's 36–6 win over UCLA. Krauss was selected by readers of 'BAMA Magazine to the Team of the '70s and was a member of the Team of the Century. He played on teams that went 31–5 and won two SEC championships and the 1978 national championship. He had 247 tackles, two interceptions, caused five fumbles, and recovered five fumbles in his Bama career. Baltimore made Krauss the sixth player taken in the 1979 NFL Draft. He played 11 years in the NFL with Baltimore, Indianapolis, and Miami.

January 1, 1993

Takeaway

"No Play" Theft by Teague Throttled Hurricanes' Hopes for Comeback

Every college football game has an official record that includes details of each play. Whoever was typing the play-by-play of the 1993 Sugar Bowl seemed to be interested in nothing beyond the bare facts. In the third quarter is this notation of Miami facing second-and-10 from its 11-yard line:

2-10 MIA 11 Alabama penalized for offsides

There was more to the play.

The Sugar Bowl game in the Louisiana Superdome pitted No. 1 Miami and Heisman Trophy–winning quarterback Gino Torretta against No. 2 Alabama for the national championship. Bama had scored two quick touchdowns in the third quarter to take a 27–6 lead. Miami had to make a move.

Lamar Thomas, the Hurricanes' outstanding wide receiver, had been widely quoted prior to the game regarding the superiority of Miami. Thomas was not having a great night; only four receptions for short yardage, no touchdowns, and one lost fumble.

But Thomas was talented and fast (a member of the Miami track team), and eventually he used a deft hip fake to blow past Alabama cornerback George Teague and Tide nickel back Willie Gaston down the Miami sideline. Torretta lofted a perfect pass and Thomas took it at the 36.

"I can tell you what was going through my mind," Teague said. "It was in big, bold letters. Fear. I didn't want to have to go to the sideline after Lamar's touchdown and face Coach Stallings. I was out of position on the play, maybe even loafing a bit."

The race was on. "I chased him out of panic," Teague said. "I think you get faster and stronger when you're scared."

If Teague catching up to Thomas was astonishing, what followed was astounding. Rather than going for the tackle, Teague went for the ball. Thomas had the ball in his right arm, to the inside of the field. Teague snatched for the ball at the 15-yard line, yanked the ball free, and at the 7-yard line Teague had possession. He returned it to the Alabama 13 where Thomas dragged him down.

George Teague ripped a ball away from Miami's Lamar Thomas and also returned an interception for a touchdown in the 1993 Sugar Bowl.

Thomas was probably faster than Teague. It took Teague 74 yards to catch Thomas. It took Thomas only six yards to catch Teague.

Bill Oliver, Alabama's secondary coach, said, "That was the darndest play. That was one of the most superb efforts a University of Alabama football player has ever made. The way he ran the guy down was unbelievable. It was the greatest individual effort I've seen."

Teague said, "Coach Oliver tells us to try to strip the ball if the receiver's not ready for it. I didn't think Thomas knew that I was right behind him. It made me feel good that I could catch a guy who runs that fast."

Even more incredibly, Alabama did not get possession of the football despite Teague's heroics. The Crimson Tide had been offside. The Hurricanes kept the ball, but they didn't get the 89-yard touchdown that seemed imminent. From an Alabama standpoint, the theft by Teague doused any hope of the Hurricanes getting back into the game.

Reports that it was not a play were inaccurate. It was a penalty play. Ironically, the penalized team was ecstatic, and the team receiving the benefit of the penalty did not reap a true reward.

"I didn't realize how big a play that was until after the game when it was all over the news," Teague said. "People wanted to do paintings of it. It's incredible to me that it happened in 1993 and it's still talked about. I was just doing my job, but it turned out to be something I am remembered for. It's better to be remembered for something positive than for something negative."

Teague's remarkable feat overshadowed his other big play in the game. Midway through the third quarter, Alabama had a 20–6 lead when Teague stepped in front of receiver Jonathan Harris on a crossing route. "The ball came right to me," Teague said. "I just wanted to get to the sideline and outrun Gino to the end zone."

That touchdown came 16 seconds after the second of two Derrick Lassic touchdown runs. Alabama had burst from a 13–6 halftime lead to a 27–6 advantage.

Surprisingly, Teague was not the MVP. That honor went to Lassic, who rushed 28 times for 135 yards and those two touchdowns.

Alabama's 12th national championship came in the Crimson Tide's 100th year of football.

Teague had one small regret. "With Torretta having won the Heisman Trophy, I had planned on striking the Heisman pose if I were to score," Teague said. "But after I scored, my teammates and I all got to celebrating and I forgot to do it. I remembered when I got to the bench, but it was too late."

Game Details

Alabama 34 • Miami 13

Miami	3	3	0	7	**13**
Alabama	3	10	14	7	**34**

Date: January 1, 1993

Team Records: Alabama 12–0, Miami 11–0

Scoring Plays:

UA Proctor 19-yard field goal
UM Prewitt 49-yard field goal
UA Proctor 23-yard field goal
UA Williams 2-yard rush (Proctor kick)
UM Prewitt 42-yard field goal
UA Lassic 1-yard rush (Proctor kick)
UA Teague 31-yard interception return (Proctor kick)
UM Williams 78-yard punt return (Prewitt kick)
UA Lassic 4-yard rush (Proctor kick)

> **T**hey dominated the football game. They deserved to win, and they deserve to be national champions.
>
> —DENNIS ERICKSON, MIAMI COACH

Bill Oliver

Bill Oliver is considered one of the outstanding defensive coaching minds of all time. He was an Alabama player under Paul Bryant, a member of Bryant's first recruiting class, and a defensive back on the 1961 national championship team. He also played baseball and was All-SEC. He coached the secondary at Auburn from 1966 to 1970, then returned to Alabama as secondary coach in 1971. Following the 1979 season, Oliver was head coach at Tennessee-Chattanooga (1980–83), defensive coordinator for the Memphis Showboats of the United States Football League (1984–85), and secondary coach at Clemson (1986–89). He returned to Alabama as secondary coach and defensive coordinator under Gene Stallings in 1990. Oliver went to Auburn as defensive coordinator in 1996 and served as head coach of the Tigers in the last part of the 1998 season after the resignation of Terry Bowden.

Bill Oliver played for Paul Bryant, coached the Alabama secondary, and also served as defensive coordinator during his long football career.

January 1, 1965

Inches Short

Joe Namath's Failure to Score Helped Tide Win Later National Championship

The very best players and the very best coaches don't win every game, but some losses are worse than others. When Alabama lost to Texas in the Orange Bowl at the end of the 1964 season, it was painful, but circumstances produced more winners than losers. Certainly Texas was a winner, and Alabama had already won the national championship, which was awarded prior to bowl games. Crimson Tide quarterback Joe Namath was definitely a winner, named Most Valuable Player in the game even though he was on the losing team.

An unintended consequence of the January 1, 1965, loss to Texas was that it set the stage for another Alabama national championship.

Alabama had some bad luck in falling behind by 21–7 at halftime. The Longhorns were leading 14–7 late in the first half and facing fourth-and-5 at the Alabama 28. An attempted field goal by David Conway was blocked by Bama end Creed Gilmer and picked up by defensive back David Ray. Ray fumbled when he was tackled and Texas had the ball back.

On the next play, Texas tried a pass, and quarterback Jim Hudson was sacked by Jim Simmons. Downfield, however, Alabama had been called for holding on Longhorns receiver George Sauer. Texas got the ball at the Alabama 13. Just before intermission, Texas running back Ernie Koy went in for what would be the winning touchdown.

Texas used two big plays for its first two touchdowns. Just before the end of the first quarter, Koy ran 79 yards. Early in the second period, Hudson completed a pass to Sauer for 69 yards.

Namath did not start the game. He had injured his knee during the season, and the injury had been aggravated in practice. Steve Sloan started, but he, too, was hobbled with a knee injury. Even though Bryant said later, "We didn't plan to play him," Namath entered the game in the first quarter.

Alabama put together an 87-yard drive that cut the lead to 14–7. Namath completed a seven-yard pass to Wayne Trimble for the touchdown.

In the third quarter, Namath got the Tide rolling. He completed passes to Tommy Tolleson, Wayne Cook, and Ray Perkins to get to the Texas 20, and then hurled a perfect strike to Perkins for the touchdown.

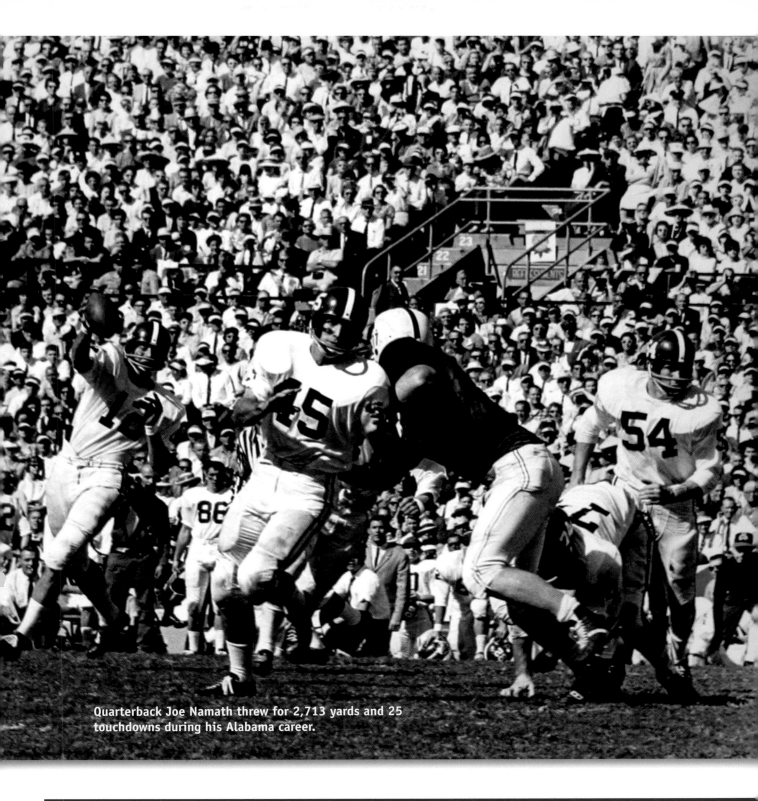

Quarterback Joe Namath threw for 2,713 yards and 25 touchdowns during his Alabama career.

Gaylon McCollough

Gaylon McCollough was a two-year starter (1963–64) at center for the Crimson Tide and was drafted by the Dallas Cowboys, but McCollough had a different ambition. He was an Academic All-American and elected to become a surgeon. He lives in Gulf Shores, Alabama, and practices at the McCollough Institute, but also travels the world sharing his skills. He is listed in "Best Doctors in America" and "America's Top Plastic Surgeons." He was personal physician to Coach Bryant. He has authored six books. In a feature article chronicling his many accomplishments, an international professional publication labeled him a "Renaissance Man."

Gaylon McCollough was a two-year starter for Paul Bryant before going on to a distinguished medical career.

A fourth-quarter drive bogged down, but David Ray kicked a 26-yard field goal to cut the Texas lead to 21–17.

The final drama came earlier than might be expected. Almost seven minutes remained when Jimmy Fuller intercepted a Texas pass and Alabama had first-and-goal at the Longhorns' 6-yard line.

On first down, fullback Steve Bowman took it up the middle for four yards. That may have been bad luck for Alabama. Had Bowman been stopped much shorter, Namath almost certainly would have passed. Instead, Bowman took two more shots at the Tommy Nobis–led Texas defense. He gained ground, but not all of the two yards. A few inches remained.

"On fourth down we went with the surest play, a quarterback sneak," Namath said. "It wasn't disrespect of Texas. It was a belief that we could knock them off the ball and get in.

"Over the years people have asked, 'Joe Willie, did you score a touchdown against Texas?' My answer is that I did not, because it was not ruled a touchdown. But I did get over the goal line. Over the years so many times have I wished that I had enough brains instead of being caught up in the situation to call timeout on third down to go over and talk to the man, talk to Coach Bryant."

Bryant would say later, "I called every play," but Namath said he had made all the calls.

No one was closer to the final play than center Gaylon McCollough. In his book, *The Long Shadow of Coach Paul "Bear" Bryant*, McCollough wrote: "On the final play of my University of Alabama career, I snapped the ball to Namath…. When the dust settled, I looked for my teammate. Joe Namath had run a quarterback sneak behind my block. It was easy to find Joe. He was lying right on top of me in the end zone."

McCollough described an official signaling touchdown, another questioning the call, and the referee deciding the ball was down inside the 1-yard line.

McCollough said the Bryant lesson that night was, "If you want to accomplish something, don't do just enough to get the job done. Go beyond what is required."

Game Details

Texas 21 • Alabama 17

Alabama	0	7	7	3	**17**
Texas	7	14	0	0	**21**

Date: January 1, 1965
Team Records: Alabama 10–0, Texas 9–1
Scoring Plays:
UT Koy 79-yard rush (Conway kick)
UT Sauer 69-yard pass from Hudson (Conway kick)
UA Trimble 7-yard pass from Namath (Ray kick)
UT Koy 1-yard rush (Conway kick)
UA Perkins 20-yard pass from Namath (Ray kick)
UA Ray 26-yard field goal

In the end, the loss to Texas precipitated a change that would benefit Alabama the following season. The Associated Press decided that since the No. 1 team had been beaten in a bowl game that followed the season, the AP would have a final poll after all the bowl games. In 1965, Alabama would not have been regular-season national champion, but when all the bowl games had been played, Bama's win over Nebraska in the Orange Bowl returned the national championship trophy to Tuscaloosa.

> **I** didn't think Joe scored afterward, because the official said he didn't. The official was right there where he could see it, and I couldn't. If you can't make a yard down there, you don't deserve to win.
>
> **—PAUL BRYANT, ALABAMA COACH**

January 1, 1966

Tackle Eligible

Lineman Catches Unlikely Pass to Help Tide Win National Title

Alabama coach Paul Bryant always enjoyed a little mischief and was not above employing a little trickery in pursuit of a victory. In 1965, Alabama trailed Mississippi 9–0 at halftime at Birmingham's Legion Field. Bama had fought back to trail by 16–10 with time running out when Bryant called for the tackle-eligible play.

Jerry Duncan was Alabama's weak-side tackle. The play involved lining up the offensive line so that no one was outside of Duncan on the line of scrimmage.

"I was scared to death," Duncan said. "We had practiced it, but we'd never used it. If I'd dropped it, they'd have run me back to North Carolina."

Duncan bumped off the defensive tackle, went out on a flare route, and quarterback Steve Sloan threw it to him. Duncan didn't drop it and picked up 17 yards. A few plays later Sloan ran in for the winning touchdown.

The 1965 season for Alabama was an unusual one with Bama, the defending national champion, having lost the season opener at Georgia and having been tied by Tennessee. Nevertheless, Bama was ranked fourth in the nation and invited to the Orange Bowl to meet third-ranked Nebraska. For the first time, the Associated Press final poll was going to be taken following bowl games. During the afternoon, top-ranked Michigan State lost to UCLA in the Rose Bowl and second-ranked Arkansas was beaten by LSU in the Cotton Bowl. The Orange Bowl, pitting giant-sized Nebraska against pint-sized Alabama, would be for the national championship.

Bryant was willing to pull out all stops against the Cornhuskers of coach Bob Devaney.

"Nebraska had giant tackles," Duncan said. "Walt Barnes, who would be a second-round draft choice of the Washington Redskins, weighed 250, and Tony Jeter was 230. That's not big today, but we were in the 160-200 range."

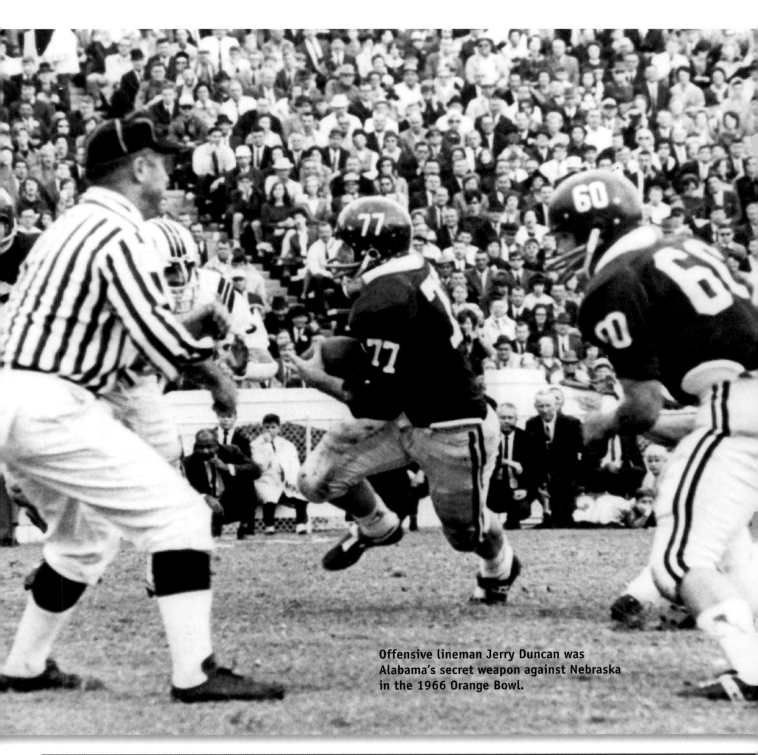

Offensive lineman Jerry Duncan was Alabama's secret weapon against Nebraska in the 1966 Orange Bowl.

Steve Sloan

Steve Sloan was Southeastern Conference Player of the Year, SEC Back of the Year, All-America, Academic All-America, and led the nation in passing efficiency as a senior in 1965. He surpassed Joe Namath's Alabama record for passing yards in a season (1,453) and exceeded Harry Gilmer's total offense mark with 1,499 yards. He completed an Alabama-record 60.6 percent of his passes as a senior. He was Most Valuable Player in the Orange Bowl as he broke Namath's record for passing yards. He would become head football coach at Vanderbilt, Texas Tech, Ole Miss, and Duke, and director of athletics at Alabama, Central Florida, and Tennessee-Chattanooga.

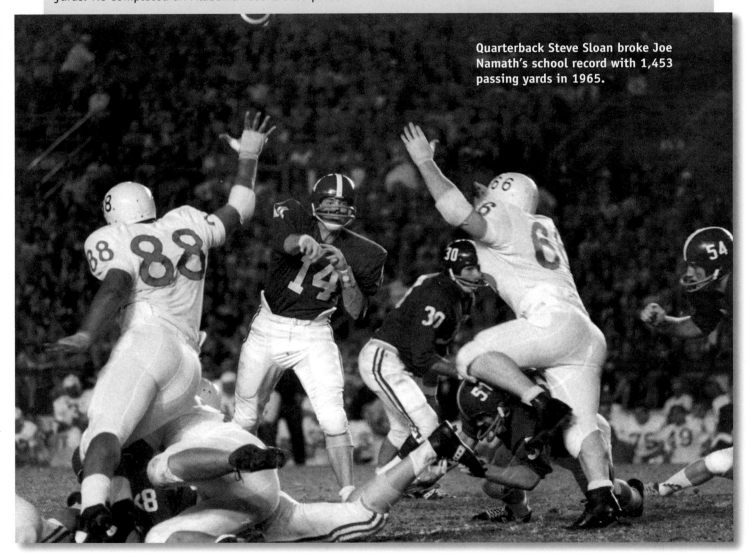

Quarterback Steve Sloan broke Joe Namath's school record with 1,453 passing yards in 1965.

Guard Johnny Calvert said, "When we had picture day in Miami before the game, Coach Bryant didn't want to pose with the offensive line because he said we were going to get the hell beat out of us. We were determined to show that so-and-so he didn't know what he was talking about."

"We ran 'tackle eligible' three times in the Orange Bowl," Duncan said. "The first time I was on the right side and we ran it as a little flare. You could do anything out of it. Nebraska had real aggressive tackles, so I'd have to hit the tackle first. Sloan would fake to the fullback, and then check for me. I slipped, which kept it from being a big gain, but still gained nine yards."

On the next play, Duncan moved to the left side and Bama ran a screen version of the same play. "On the screen, you really had to hold the tackles up," Duncan said. "Trying to hold up Walt Barnes was like trying to slow down a freight train. But we all held our men, and Sloan made a perfect pass and gained about 17 yards."

Duncan caught three passes for 32 yards.

Devaney said, "We knew we had to stop Sloan, so we gambled by putting on a good rush, but we didn't get to him. They used that tackle-eligible screen very effectively."

Bryant said, "We've been lining up for that all year, but we only did it once during the [regular] season. I think we caught Nebraska off balance with it. Duncan grabbed those passes like an end, didn't he?"

Bryant said later, "I told Steve before the game, 'Steve, we're not going to win the national championship by lucking out 7–6 or something like that. We have to win big. I don't care where you are on the field or what the score is, I want you to play like you're behind.'"

At the half, Alabama had a 24–7 lead, primarily because of Sloan's passing. The Tide switched to a ground game in the second half and went on to a 39–28 decision that wasn't as close as the final score.

Sloan, who suffered torn cartilage in his rib cage, set an Orange Bowl record by completing 20 passes in 28 attempts for 296 yards and two touchdowns.

Ole Miss coach John Vaught, the man who had been the victim of the tackle-eligible play earlier in the year, used his spot on the college football rules committee to have the play deemed illegal. And with the rule change implemented after the next season, the last tackle-eligible pass in college football was thrown by Ken Stabler to Jerry Duncan in the 1967 Sugar Bowl against Nebraska.

> **If** I had a vote, I would certainly vote for us. I don't believe any team in America would have beaten us Saturday night, but you sportswriters will have to decide.
>
> —PAUL BRYANT, ALABAMA COACH

Game Details

Alabama 39 • Nebraska 28

Alabama	7	17	8	7	**39**
Nebraska	0	7	6	15	**28**

Date: January 1, 1966
Team Records: Alabama 8–1–1, Nebraska 10–0
Scoring Plays:
UA Perkins 21-yard pass from Sloan (Ray kick)
NU Jeter 33-yard pass from Churchich (Wachholtz kick)
UA Kelley 4-yard run (Ray kick)
UA Perkins 11-yard pass from Sloan (Ray kick)
UA Ray 18-yard field goal
NU Gregory 49-yard pass from Churchich (pass failed)
UA Bowman 1-yard run (Perkins pass from Sloan)
NU Churchich 1-yard run (Wachholtz kick)
UA Bowman 3-yard run (Ray kick)
NU Jeter 14-yard pass from Churchich (Gregory pass from Churchich)

January 2, 1967

The Perfect Beginning to a Perfect End

Snake Stabler and Ray Perkins Assured Tide Would Be 11–0

Alabama halfback Les Kelley had a long jog after the first play of the 1967 Sugar Bowl. Kenny Stabler had completed a 45-yard pass to Ray Perkins. As Kelley and his Crimson Tide teammates, along with players from Nebraska, made their way downfield, a Nebraska defender muttered to Kelley, "Here we go again." The Nebraska player had spent the night of January 1, 1966, chasing Bama players in the Tide's 39–28 Orange Bowl victory.

Nebraska coach Bob Devaney tried to warn the Cornhuskers.

"The first play didn't surprise us," Devaney said. "In our sideline huddle prior to the first play, I said, 'Watch Perkins.' However, Perkins was just too fast. Kaye Carstens is our fastest defensive back. He let Perkins get a step on him and Stabler happened to throw a perfect pass."

Kenny Stabler "happened" to throw a lot of perfect passes in his Crimson Tide career, and the left-handed quarterback tossed a dart on the first play of the 1967 Sugar Bowl. Nebraska never recovered.

Alabama coach Paul Bryant called the first-down play. "We wanted to throw long to Perkins to see what defense they were in," Bryant said. "If Perkins was covered, Stabler was to overthrow. Perkins got behind them, though, and that really gave us an early lift."

Quarterback Ken "the Snake" Stabler led the Tide past Nebraska in the 1967 Sugar Bowl.

Stabler said, "The coaches decided that if we won the toss and received the kickoff and got good field position, we would try the bomb on the very first play. I sent Ray down the left side on what we call a 'go' route. He just ran under control for about 10 yards, faked inside, and took off. I had all day to throw the ball. I put it high in the air, and Perkins was right there." That pass went for 45 yards, from the Tide 28 to Nebraska's 27. Perkins caught it at the 40 and ran 13 more yards before being tackled.

Nebraska halfback Harry Wilson said, "Alabama didn't let us do much of anything. They just had too much speed for us. I guess they broke our backs with that long pass at the start."

Seven plays after the game-opening pass from Stabler to Perkins, Kelly went in for a touchdown and the rout was under way. Alabama led 17–0 at the end of the first quarter and 24–0 at halftime. Steve Davis kicked his second field goal in the third quarter. Nebraska finally got on the scoreboard on the fourth play of the fourth quarter.

Nebraska quarterback Bob Churchich said, "I wasn't able to mix up my plays because we were so far behind. The only way to get back in the game was to put the ball in the air." That was not good, either. Bobby Johns had three interceptions, and Bob Childs and Stan Moss one each.

Alabama won 34–7. The Crimson Tide was unbeaten and untied, but also uncrowned. Bama's seniors had won two national championships and had a record of 30–2–1. (An astounding testament to Alabama's disciplined play is that the Tide did not have a single holding penalty in 1965 or 1966.)

Devaney said, "Alabama is several touchdowns better than the team that beat us last year, and we knew that as soon as we studied the films. Today, Alabama was a much better team than we were, and the score showed it.

"Stabler was just too quick for the people we had chasing him. Perkins is the finest collegiate receiver I've ever seen. We tried to double-cover on both sides, but then they'd run on us. They were as fine a college football team as I have ever seen."

Stabler won the Miller-Digby Trophy as the game's Most Valuable Player. Perkins finished second.

Bryant said, "This club had everything—great defense, great offense, and leadership from its seniors. It also had two of the finest receivers I've ever seen in Ray Perkins and Dennis Homan."

Game Details

Alabama 34 • Nebraska 7

Alabama	17	7	3	7	**34**
Nebraska	0	0	0	7	**7**

Date: January 2, 1967
Team Records: Alabama 10–0, Nebraska 9–1
Scoring Plays:
UA Kelly 1-yard rush (S. Davis kick)
UA Stabler 14-yard rush (S. Davis kick)
UA S. Davis 30-yard field goal
UA Trimble 6-yard rush (S. Davis kick)
UA S. Davis 40-yard field goal
NU D. Davis 15-yard pass from Churchich (Wachholtz kick)
UA Perkins 45-yard pass from Stabler (S. Davis kick)

> **O**ur players started back last January planning to make this a perfect season for us. This is the greatest college football team I've ever been associated with. It is the greatest college team I've seen, too, and they proved it today. They deserve to be No. 1, and if I had a vote, they would be.
>
> **—PAUL BRYANT, ALABAMA COACH**

Ray Perkins

Ray Perkins was an All-American in 1966 and was captain of that undefeated Crimson Tide team. He was selected to the Alabama Team of the Decade for the 1960s. He set an Alabama bowl record with nine receptions in the 1966 Orange Bowl and set another record with 178 yards in the 1967 Sugar Bowl. The 178 receiving yards broke the record of 164 set by Don Hutson in the 1935 Rose Bowl. Perkins played in two Super Bowls for the Baltimore Colts, the first one under coach Don Shula. Shula's son Mike would be quarterback for Alabama under Perkins. Perkins was head coach in the NFL with Tampa Bay and the New York Giants and in college at Alabama (1983–86), following Paul Bryant, and at Arkansas State.

Ray Perkins' 178 receiving yards, including his 45-yard reception on the Tide's opening play, set a Sugar Bowl record.

Kenny Stabler should be everybody's All-American next year.

—RAY PERKINS, ALABAMA SPLIT END

Heart-Stoppers

December 2, 1967

Run in the Mud

Snake Stabler's Amazing Run Overcame Elements and Auburn

Auburn linebacker Gusty Yearout was friends with several Alabama football players. In the summer he worked out with Tide tailback Frank Canterbury at Ramsay High School in Birmingham, where the two had been teammates. Yearout was Auburn captain and went to midfield for the coin toss. Quarterback Kenny Stabler represented the Alabama seniors, who all served as captains for the Auburn game.

"Back then the coaches taught you to hate the opponent," Yearout said. "I was intense and competitive anyway, so I had worked up a real hate for Alabama going into the game. As we went out for the coin toss, I put on the meanest, hardest look I could. I meant to intimidate Stabler from the start. I was trying to stare Stabler down, the referee was trying to introduce the captains, and Stabler was talking.

"He said, 'Hey, Gusty. What are y'all doing after the game? We're having a party at the Bankhead [Hotel]. We've got plenty of beer. Y'all come on over.'"

"I guess it made me mad that my intimidation wasn't working," Yearout said. "Finally I stammered, 'What room?'"

The level of celebration by Stabler is not recorded, but it's safe to say that he was being toasted by a host of Alabama followers. Alabama had defeated Auburn 7–3 because of one magnificent run in almost impossible conditions. A heavy rain in Birmingham had turned Legion Field into a sea of mud. The field was used throughout the fall for college and high school games, and by December 2 there was scarcely a blade of grass.

Presumably some spectators left the stadium early, but the vast majority stayed to the end. The rain was unpleasant and inconvenient. Tornados in the area could have proved disastrous.

Alabama eschewed the pass for most of the day. Stabler, one of the most effective passers in the nation, threw only five times, completing three for a mere 12 yards. Alabama had only five first downs and total offense of only 176 yards. Indeed, Alabama had only one meaningful offensive play, but that was enough.

Field conditions were a factor from the opening kickoff. Literally. Alabama elected to kick off, but Tide defenders were slipping and sliding. Eddie Propst made a touchdown-saving tackle for the Tide.

Ken Stabler's touchdown run against Auburn in 1967 is one of the most memorable moments in Alabama history.

Auburn's problems with its kicking game were instrumental in Alabama's win. The Tigers got close to the Alabama goal line five times, but managed only a third-quarter field goal by John Riley for all their efforts. One first-half Auburn field-goal try sailed wide to the right; another was short due to a poor snap.

As a result, Auburn made two questionable coaching decisions. In the second quarter, Auburn was faced with a fourth-and-goal at the Alabama 3-yard line and tried to run but was stopped at the 1. Later in the half the Tigers tried a run on fourth-and-2 at the Alabama 7, and again the attempt failed.

Other Auburn errors played a role in Alabama's victory. Early in the fourth quarter, an apparent Auburn first down at the Bama 15 was wiped out by a penalty. Moments later the Tigers were forced to punt. The Auburn punter was

Ken Stabler

Kenny "the Snake" Stabler was an All-American in 1967. He played on teams that compiled a 28–3–2 record (1965–67) including a perfect 11–0 mark in 1966. He was winner of the Miller-Digby Trophy as Most Valuable Player of the Sugar Bowl as he completed 12 of 17 passes for 218 yards and rushed for 40 yards in a 34–7 win over Nebraska. He was SEC Player of the Year. He and Joe Namath were selected as quarterbacks of Alabama's Team of the Century. Stabler was selected by Oakland in the second round of the AFL-NFL Draft. He had been a second-round Major League Baseball draft pick by the Houston Astros, but turned that down for the NFL. He spent his 15-year NFL career with Oakland, Houston, and New Orleans. He was the winning quarterback in Super Bowl XI. He served as color man on radio broadcasts of Alabama football.

Ken Stabler passed for nearly 2,200 yards in his Alabama career and led the 1966 team to an 11–0 undefeated season.

It still amazes me the number of people who will tell me about seeing the run in the mud. The details of the rain and wind, umbrellas turned inside out, clothes ruined, and yet they stayed to watch. I hear this virtually every day from some Alabama fan. I listen to the whole story because it is a thrill for them and it is a great feeling for me that they remember.

—KEN STABLER, ALABAMA QUARTERBACK

unable to handle a low snap and had to fall on the ball, giving it to Alabama at the Tide 46.

Halfback Tommy Wade went at left end for five yards, then up the middle for two to the Auburn 47. On third-and-3, Stabler called an option right. There was, however, no option.

"They had been making me run all day," Stabler said of the Auburn defense. "I made up my mind there would be no pitch. I was going to run that one."

Run he did. He picked up blocks at the corner by tight end Dennis Dixon and fullback David Chatwood, and as he made his way downfield, Stabler pointed out a target for Dennis Homan. Homan made the block.

Stabler, a left-hander, carried the ball in his right arm, away from his pursuers. He directed blockers with his left hand. His run went down the Alabama sideline and into the end zone. Steve Davis kicked the extra point. It was Alabama's longest running play of the season and the longest run in Stabler's career.

"Give Dennis Homan credit for most of it," Stabler said. "He threw the big block. All I did was run."

There was still 11:29 remaining in the game, but considering the conditions, an Auburn touchdown was unlikely. Alabama linebacker Bob Childs intercepted two Auburn passes in the final minutes, and Davis had a key punt for Alabama, a 55-yard effort that went to the Auburn 6.

Punting had been a strategic weapon for the Tide. When Alabama had the wind in the fourth quarter and trailed only 3–0, Bryant said he thought Alabama would win. "I didn't think anyone was going to put together a long drive under those circumstances, so we kept kicking on third down," he said. "I thought for a while there I might have played it too close to the vest, but I guess the percentages haven't changed."

Bama punted throughout the game. "We punted on third down when we had the wind, because the punt was our best weapon," Bryant explained. "We waited until fourth down against the wind because we didn't want Auburn to

Game Details

Alabama 7 • Auburn 3

Alabama	0	0	0	7	**7**
Auburn	0	0	3	0	**3**

Date: December 2, 1967
Team Records: Alabama 7–1–1, Auburn 6–3
Scoring Plays:
AU Riley 38-yard field goal
UA Stabler 47-yard rush (Davis kick)

have the ball with the wind at its back. I think everybody on both sides tried as hard as they could. There were lots of big plays. But the prettiest one I saw was Stabler's run."

Alabama would go to the Cotton Bowl to play Texas A&M. An interesting guest on Alabama's sideline for the Auburn game was Gene Stallings. Stallings had played and coached for Bryant at Texas A&M, been an assistant coach at Alabama, and was head coach of the Aggies. In 1990 he would be head coach at Alabama.

A day after the game there would be a complaint from Auburn coach Ralph Jordan that Dixon had "tackled" Yearout on Stabler's touchdown run. Bryant said he didn't see that. "If there was holding, it should have been called," he said. "But I wasn't officiating."

> **I**'ve been around long enough to know that the only thing that counts is what you read on the scoreboard lights. But I don't think the best team won.
>
> **—RALPH JORDAN, AUBURN COACH**

December 5, 1992

Deception Interception

Antonio Langham Made First SEC Championship Game an Instant Legend

In 1992 the Southeastern Conference took advantage of an NCAA provision allowing a championship game if the league had at least 12 members and two divisions. The motive was money, additional millions of dollars for the participating teams and the SEC office.

Prophets of doom conjectured the extra game against a tough opponent would cost an SEC team a national championship. Late in the fourth quarter of the inaugural game, that dire prediction loomed ominous. Alabama was ranked second in the nation with an 11–0 record, but the Crimson Tide was in a struggle with the Florida Gators.

The score was tied 21–21 with just over three minutes to play. The Gators had the ball at the 21 in their own territory. Steve Spurrier–coached Florida teams were explosive, capable of moving downfield quickly. The Gators wanted to get into position for the winning score. If Florida couldn't score, the game would go to overtime.

The SEC champion was going to the Sugar Bowl. If Alabama won, it would be going to play No. 1 Miami for the national championship. If Florida won, all SEC coaches would be wondering if this championship game was a good idea for the league.

Shane Matthews was an excellent quarterback for Florida, and he had been very effective against the Crimson Tide without throwing deep passes. The call on first down was a quick 'out' route to receiver Monty Duncan. If Matthews felt Duncan was covered, he had an option to hit a secondary receiver over the middle.

"I thought I could pop it for five yards," Matthews said. "When I threw it, I didn't see Langham. He just jumped in front of Monty and made a good play."

It was more than a "good play" to Antonio Langham. "This is a player's dream come true," he said. "I wanted to make a play and carry my load."

Langham, an All-America cornerback, had been challenged by his position coach, Bill Oliver, as Alabama took the field late in the fourth quarter. "Coach Oliver told us the defense had to do something, that somebody had to make a big play," Langhorn said.

Antonio Langham's fourth-quarter interception gave Alabama the victory in the inaugural SEC Championship Game in 1992.

If I were a betting man, I'd bet 10–1 that Shane Matthews has never thrown an interception on that route. The degree of difficulty on that play Antonio Langham made in terms of a diver is a 10. Antonio's a great football player. He made the play.

—BILL OLIVER, ALABAMA DEFENSIVE COORDINATOR

Though Duncan appeared open to Matthews, Langham was right behind the receiver, waiting for his chance. Langham stepped in front of Duncan as the ball was thrown.

"They had been running that route all day, with the guy running a hitch pattern," Langham said. "I kind of eased in behind the receiver when he made the release and came around him. I broke on it when I saw the ball coming. The ball hit me right in the hands. It was history after that."

History, indeed.

Langham was in full stride from the Florida 27, headed for the end zone.

After the game, Langham said, "I knew I couldn't outrun Shane Matthews [who had an angle], so I cut back inside. I got a block, and all I saw was an offensive lineman, and I knew I could outrun him." It wasn't really that close. A couple of Gators waved at Langham, but he wasn't touched until he reached the crowd of well-wishers leaning over from the end-zone seats.

Game Details

Alabama 28 • Florida 21

Alabama	7	7	7	7	28
Florida	7	0	7	7	21

Date: December 5, 1992

Team Records: Alabama 11–0, Florida 8–3

Scoring Plays:

UF Rhett 5-yard pass from Matthews (Davis kick)

UA Lassic 5-yard rush (Proctor kick)

UA Brown 30-yard pass from Barker (Proctor kick)

UA Lassic 15-yard rush (Proctor kick)

UF Jackson 4-yard pass from Matthews (Davis kick)

UF Rhett 1-yard rush (Davis kick)

UA Langham 27-yard interception return (Proctor kick)

Langham speculated, "If I hadn't squatted down, he probably would have run a post route and completed the pass."

There was still some time, but Bama's second interception of the day allowed the Crimson Tide to ice the game in frigid Legion Field. Linebacker Michael Rogers picked off a batted Matthews pass and Bama was able to run out the clock.

Alabama had a 28–21 victory, the Tide's 22nd straight win since a 35–0 loss to Florida in Gainesville in 1991.

Alabama coach Gene Stallings said, "We've had a knack for making the big defensive play all year, and we made another one. I wouldn't have thought we would have given up 21 points, but when we had to stop them we did. Antonio is a big play kind of player."

Offensively, Alabama's reputation was as a running team, and the Gators were prepared to stop the run. Quarterback Jay Barker had a good day, completing 10 of 18 passes for 154 yards, including a 30-yard touchdown pass to Curtis Brown. David Palmer caught five balls for 101 yards. Derrick Lassic was the game's top rusher with 21 carries for 117 yards and two touchdowns.

Safety Chris Donnelly topped Tide tacklers with nine stops. Langham was among a handful of Bama players with eight tackles. Langham also broke up one pass in his MVP performance.

One important point: after Alabama's third touchdown, the Tide was hit with back-to-back penalties, a 15-yard penalty for a face-mask violation and a five-yard penalty for illegal procedure. The usually routine point-after-touchdown kick had become a 45-yard effort, but Michael Proctor kicked it through.

Alabama was off to New Orleans to play Miami for the national championship. No one gave Bama much of a chance in that one, but Stallings said, "I like our team." He said he liked that Bama was No. 1 in the nation in rushing defense and total defense and second in passing defense and scoring defense. His players would make their coach a prophet, beating the favored Hurricanes 34–13.

Derrick Lassic

After a redshirt season in 1988 and three years as a backup tailback, Derrick Lassic was an All-SEC tailback in 1992, his senior season. Lassic won the Miller-Digby Award as the Most Valuable Player in the Sugar Bowl as Bama defeated Miami for the national championship. Lassic had 28 carries for 135 yards and two touchdowns in the Sugar Bowl. As a senior,

he had 178 rushes for 905 yards (5.1 per carry) and 10 touchdowns, and caught 14 passes for 129 yards and a touchdown. He rushed for 117 yards and two touchdowns in the SEC Championship Game and was ABC Player of the Game. He was drafted by the Dallas Cowboys and played for the Cowboys in 1993–94 and for the Carolina Panthers in 1995.

Derrick Lassic rushed for 117 yards and two touchdowns against the Gators.

September 10, 2005

The Catch

Tyrone Prothro Set the Bar High with Behind-the-Back Catch

Great pass receptions are an everyday part of football and a staple of *SportsCenter* highlights. One-handed grabs, falling-down catches, leaping-high receptions, and on and on and on. But there has been only one catch like the one Tyrone Prothro made. It was so good that it continues to be a highlight years after Prothro's career has ended. It was phenomenal. It was The Catch.

The first time Prothro saw the catch was when he went to the football offices the day after the game against Southern Miss. He saw the Alabama coaching video of the play. No crowd roar. No announcers going berserk. No rerun after rerun, no slow motion, no shot from the goal post or blimp. Just what's known as a cut-up: the play from snap to finish.

"It was pretty good," Prothro agreed. "I don't know how I did it myself. I just stuck my hands out there, and the ball fell right in my hands. The ball was behind the DB, and I had to reach around him and grab it. When it hit my hand, I knew I

had my arms around the DB, and he was going to try to do anything to get it out. I was squeezing it as hard as I could, so it wouldn't come out. I held it against his back. I didn't have time to think about flipping into the end zone. It was over in a second."

The acrobatic reception would have been amazing at any time. In fact, Alabama was in a desperate situation just before halftime. The Crimson Tide had fallen behind 21–10, and Bama faced fourth-and-12 at the Southern Miss 43-yard line. Coach Mike Shula decided to risk a big play.

Southern Miss had split its safeties, leaving the middle open. "I actually couldn't believe they let Pro run down the middle like that," Alabama quarterback Brodie Croyle said. "They hadn't shown that coverage before. As soon as I set up, I uncorked it, and the rest is one of the top plays on *SportsCenter*. It was actually good coverage. Prothro just made one heck of a catch."

Prothro was guarded closely by Southern Miss defensive back Jasper Faulk. No one could

Tyrone Prothro's miraculous catch against Southern Miss inspired the Tide's come-from-behind 30–21 victory.

Tyrone Prothro

Tyrone Prothro was All-SEC in 2005 despite playing in only five games. One could hardly have had more impact in such a short time. His reception against Southern Miss was selected as the ESPN Play of the Year. In those first five games of his junior year, the 5'8", 178-pound wide receiver had 17 pass receptions for 325 yards and three touchdowns, seven kickoff returns for 193 yards, 92 yards rushing, and 81 yards on punt returns for 691 all-purpose yards. As a sophomore he became the seventh player in Alabama history to return a kickoff 100 yards for a touchdown. For the year he had 17 kickoff returns for 452 yards, leading the SEC. For his career, a total of 26 games, he had 58 receptions for 863 yards and five touchdowns, 29 kickoff returns for 774 yards, and 1,982 all-purpose yards.

Tyrone Prothro's circus grab earned him the 2006 ESPY Award for Best Play.

Game Details

Alabama 30 • Southern Miss 21

Southern Miss	14	7	0	0	**21**
Alabama	10	7	6	7	**30**

Date: September 10, 2005

Team Records: Alabama 1–0, Southern Miss 0–0

Scoring Plays:

UA Hall 26-yard pass from Croyle (Christensen kick)

UA Christensen 33-yard field goal

USM McRath 32-yard interception return (McCaleb kick)

USM Perine 12-yard pass from Almond (McCaleb kick)

USM Perine 37-yard pass from Almond (McCaleb kick)

UA McClain 1-yard pass from Croyle (Christensen kick)

UA Castille 2-yard rush (kick failed)

UA Castille 2-yard rush (Christensen kick)

fault his play, even though he was called for a dubious pass interference penalty. Faulk ran step-for-step with Prothro to inside the 10-yard line. The ball was thrown over both players' heads, but with a high arc so that it had a steep descent.

Fortunately, it was the first year the SEC used replay officials to confirm or overrule officials on the field. One official ruled touchdown, but Prothro had obviously been down outside the end zone before his lower body fell over the goal line. A second official ruled incomplete pass. The replay official was able to sort it out. Completed pass, down at the 1-yard line.

On first down, Croyle passed to fullback Le'Ron McClain for the touchdown, and Alabama had cut the Southern Miss lead to 21–17. The Tide would ride the momentum of The Catch to 13 points in the second half while the Bama defense shut down the Southerners for a 30–21 victory.

"We see him make fabulous catches in practice," Croyle said. "We're like, 'How in the world did he do that?' almost every day. But that one was truly incredible."

"I didn't know where the ball was," wide receiver D.J. Hall said. "I could see Pro and the DB hugging, but I couldn't find the ball. I thought it was an incomplete pass. Then I saw Prothro turn around with the ball in his hand and I'm like, 'Did he just make that catch?'"

Prothro had an excellent game. In his first career start, he caught seven passes for 134 yards, returned two kickoffs for 97 yards, ran back four punts for 34 yards, and rushed twice for 14 yards, a total of 279 all-purpose yards. That was second-best in Bama history behind Siran Stacy's 317 against Tennessee in 1989.

In a key Southeastern Conference game three weeks after the Southern Miss contest, Prothro had another memorable pass reception. On the first offensive play of Alabama's second drive, working from the left side, he broke past the cornerback and outran the safety. Brodie Croyle made a perfect pass and Prothro went 87 yards for a touchdown. Alabama went on to a 31–3 rout of the Gators. Later in the game, Prothro leaped for a pass in the end zone. He didn't catch the ball, and when he came down, it was awkwardly. His leg snapped. It was considered a season-ending injury. It turned out to be career ending. He never caught another pass.

Tyrone Prothro's greatest catch, however, lives on in video. It can be seen throughout the football season in any year. It will always be The Catch.

> **B**y Saturday night he had a new nickname: ESPY. A catch like that? You knew he was going to be on ESPN's plays of the week, the year, the whatever. It was amazing.
>
> —D.J. HALL, ALABAMA WIDE RECEIVER

Mike Shula and Al Bell would hook up on a 17-yard touchdown pass with 15 seconds left to beat Georgia in 1985.

September 2, 1985

Quick Strike

Mike Shula and Al Bell Complete Miracle Comeback in Athens

Chris Mohr had dreamed of playing football in Sanford Stadium. A native of Thomson, Georgia, less than an hour from Athens, Mohr was a redshirt freshman punter for Alabama. He had committed to Georgia while in high school, but when the Bulldogs didn't have a scholarship for him, Mohr went to Alabama instead.

Now, in his first college game he was in Georgia's stadium, but living a nightmare.

Selected for Labor Day Monday night television, one of the dullest football games imaginable was winding down. Alabama had hoped to win with its running game and defense, and had been successful, controlling the clock for 36 of the elapsed 59 minutes.

"Our game plan was simply to run, and I thought the players did a good job of that," Alabama coach Ray Perkins explained. "I don't look at it in terms of conservative or wide-open. I look at it as just good, tough, aggressive offense."

Mohr was deep in his territory when he took his last snap of the night. Line blocking was not good and Mohr was not quick. Georgia linebacker Terrie Webster broke through and blocked the punt. Poor Southeastern Conference officiating may have worked to Alabama's benefit, though it can never be known. Calvin Ruff swatted the ball toward the goal line (illegal batting was not called), and Ruff fell on the ball in the end zone for a touchdown. With the extra-point kick, Georgia had its first lead of the game at 16–13. Fifty seconds remained.

The understandable Georgia celebration was both premature and costly.

The Bulldogs were hit with an unsportsmanlike celebration penalty and had to kick off from the 25-yard line. Alabama had reasonable starting field position at its 29.

"What was I thinking?" Perkins said. "I was thinking we had 50 seconds to get into position and we had no timeouts. It's one of those exciting-type things a coach can do without. I was thinking about a field goal when we got in range. If it came down to it, and I saw we didn't have a last shot to score a touchdown, I wasn't going to let my team walk out of here losers. They didn't deserve that."

Mike Shula

Mike Shula is football royalty, the son of Don Shula, one of the greatest coaches in NFL history. Mike made his first mark in 1985 as an All-Southeastern Conference quarterback for Alabama. He was a three-year letterman and starter (1984–86) as quarterback for the Crimson Tide and had a record of 24–11–1. He completed 313 of 578 passes for 4,069 yards and 35 touchdowns and ranks among Alabama all-time passing leaders. He was winner of the Paul Bryant Award as The University's top student-athlete. He was drafted by Tampa Bay and had a brief pro playing career, but has made his mark as a coach. He was an assistant coach in the NFL before becoming head coach at Alabama in 2003. He had a four-year record of 26–23. He returned to the NFL as an assistant coach after leaving Alabama.

Quarterback Mike Shula was All-SEC in 1985; he returned to the Tide as head coach in 2003.

Game Details

Alabama 20 • Georgia 16

Alabama	0	7	3	10	**20**
Georgia	0	3	0	13	**16**

Date: September 2, 1985
Team Records: Alabama 0–0, Georgia 0–0
Scoring Plays:
UA Bell 16-yard pass from Shula (Tiffin kick)
UG Crumley 48-yard field goal
UA Tiffin 48-yard field goal
UA Tiffin 41-yard field goal
UG Hockaday 11-yard pass from Johnson (pass failed)
UG Ruff recovered blocked punt in end zone (Crumley kick)
UA Bell 17-yard pass from Shula (Tiffin kick)

The game plan had changed. The outcome depended on the strong left arm of quarterback Mike Shula.

Alabama almost made it a one-play comeback. Tailback Kerry Goode slipped out of the backfield and down the left sideline behind the coverage. Shula saw him and threw, but the pass was barely long, just out of Goode's reach.

Georgia coaches would say later they used four different coverages on the next four plays. None worked. "It wasn't like we just sat there and let them score on that last drive," said Georgia defensive coordinator Bill Lewis. "We tried to mix things up with the blitz and zone, but Shula did a good job finding the holes in the zone. They anticipated the blitz real well."

One sack or even one rushed pass might have been fatal to the Alabama comeback, but the Alabama line allowed no pressure on Shula from the Georgia rush.

Georgia coach Vince Dooley said, "When the chips were down, Shula looked very poised. We couldn't put any pressure on him. He just stood back there with poise, and picked us apart. We were tired. The defense had been on the field too long. We couldn't get a pass rush out of anybody."

Shula completed a pass to split end Greg Richardson for a first down at the Alabama 45. Shula threw to flanker Al Bell, who made a leaping, one-handed grab for 26 yards. Shula went back to Richardson for 17 yards to the Georgia 17.

Bell, playing in his first Alabama game, ran "a simple post pattern," he said. "I took the safety on the outside and he fell for it, leaving me open in the middle. The ball was right there." With 15 seconds to play, Shula's pass to Bell gave Alabama the lead. Van Tiffin's kick completed the scoring at 20–16.

"They had one-on-one coverage on Albert and I wanted to get the ball to him," Shula said. "He has great hands, great speed, and great concentration. He's one of those guys who can make a quarterback look good."

Perkins said, "Anytime we call on Al Bell, he does the job. He's got everything you want a receiver to have; an awful lot of ability."

The 71-yard touchdown drive had taken five plays and used only 35 seconds. Five of Shula's 13 passes, four of his nine completions, and 71 of his 136 passing yards had come in the game-winning march. Bell had four receptions for 77 yards and two touchdowns.

On the Alabama bench, freshman punter Chris Mohr had composed himself just in time to see the heroics of his teammates. Mohr had been wiping tears from his face with a towel. "I got down on myself and almost missed the ending," he said. "I couldn't believe what happened."

Sometimes dreams really do come true.

> **S**hula did exactly what he had to do to win in the first 50 minutes, playing the way he was supposed to. And then, when things got out of hand, he played the other way, doing what he had to do to win. He's a winner.
>
> **—VINCE DOOLEY, GEORGIA COACH**

October 2, 1999

Win in the Swamp

Shaun Alexander Runs Behind Chris Samuels for Upset of Gators

How many times does a football team give up 39 points and win? It happened in an unlikely venue as Alabama went into Ben Hill Griffin Stadium in Gainesville and came away with a 40–39 overtime victory over the Florida Gators. Coach Steve Spurrier's squad had a 30-game winning streak on its home field and the Gators were 4–0 and ranked third in the nation. Alabama's record, on the other hand, included a loss to…Louisiana Tech.

Florida fans were understandably frustrated as Alabama kept the Florida offense on the sideline much of the day. Bama had the football for 41:22 to just 18:38 for the Gators before the teams went to overtime. The game was tied only twice—at 0–0 when it started and at 33–33 when regulation time ended. In between there were nine lead changes.

Florida had done a very good job defending the potent running game of Tide tailback Shaun Alexander. But Alexander could be contained only so long. He scored the touchdowns that gave Alabama a chance to win.

Alabama won the coin toss to begin overtime and elected to go on defense first. The Tide surrendered a touchdown to Florida, but the Gators missed the extra point and held a 39–33 lead. The Gators were already kicking themselves over a critical error earlier in the kicking game. With just 3:30 to play and Florida holding a 33–26 lead, Bama had to punt. The Florida punt returner fumbled the ball and Bama's Marvin Brown came out of a huge stack of football humanity with the ball.

Brown gave an assist to defensive end Kindal Moorehead. "When you're in the pile, you do whatever you have to do to get the football," Brown said. "I got a little scratched up trying to take it away from the Florida guy who had it. I was pulling on it and Kindal was punching at the ball from the other side. Once I had it, Kindal turned the pile over so the ref could see I had the ball."

Florida was to have yet another error in a kicking situation.

Alabama got the ball at the 25 to start its possession in overtime. Crimson Tide offensive coordinator Charlie Stubbs said running backs coach Ivy Williams suggested the first-down call. It was never unusual for

> **T**hey're still hollering out there, and we're crying.
> That's the way sports is. The winner laughs, the loser
> cries, and one or two plays make the difference.
>
> —STEVE SPURRIER, FLORIDA COACH

Shaun Alexander rushed for 106 yards and three touchdowns to tame the Gators in Gainesville in 1999.

Chris Samuels

Chris Samuels was Alabama's first Outland Trophy winner as the nation's best lineman in 1999. He won the Jacobs Award as the best blocker in the Southeastern Conference and was selected the SEC's top offensive lineman. Samuels was a consensus All-American at left tackle. He started 42 consecutive games for Bama. He was redshirted in 1995 and became a starter midway through the 1996 season. He did not give up a sack or a quarterback pressure as a senior. Following his Alabama career he was selected third overall in the 2000 NFL Draft by the Washington Redskins. He was selected for the Pro Bowl on numerous occasions. In 2008 he was reunited with Shaun Alexander when Alexander joined the Redskins.

Offensive tackle Chris Samuels blocked for Shaun Alexander and won the Outland Trophy in 1999.

tailback Shaun Alexander to run behind left tackle Chris Samuels. Samuels was considered the best lineman in the Southeastern Conference, perhaps the nation. Instead of the normal off-tackle dive, though, Alabama went to a counter play, hoping to neutralize Florida's quick pursuit.

Tide quarterback Andrew Zow and Alexander feinted right, and then came back left. Alexander took the pitch and cut behind a block by Samuels. Downfield, tight end Shaun Draper provided a crushing block that took out two Gators and sprung Alexander for the final 10 yards and a 39–39 tie. Prior to that sprint, Florida had held Alexander to 81 yards on 27 carries.

"I wasn't doing a thing," Alexander said. "I told 'Big Sam' that he and the other offensive linemen were getting the job done. They were refusing to lose."

Alabama coach Mike DuBose also had praise for the offensive line. "Our ability to establish the run and mix in passes was strictly because our offensive line handled Florida's speed on defense," DuBose said. "Our offensive line gives Shaun room to make a play every time he touches the football."

After the touchdown, all that was left was a routine kick for the winning point.

Regular place-kicker Ryan Pflugner was out with an injury and Florida native Chris Kemp was handling those chores. Earlier in the game, Kemp had kicked two field goals (37 yards and 22 yards) and three extra points in three tries. This time he missed.

Florida, however, made yet another kicking-game mistake; the Gators were offside. Kemp got another chance and nailed it.

After the game, Mike DuBose was asked about the winning touchdown play. "We call it 'Watch No. 37 Play,'" the Tide coach joked.

Alexander—No. 37 himself—had 28 carries for 106 yards and three touchdowns, including a 13-yard run on fourth-and-2 that sent the game to overtime. Alexander caught four passes for 94 yards, including one for a 47-yard touchdown. Andrew Zow enjoyed his finest day passing at The Capstone, as the redshirt sophomore threw for 336 yards on 28 of 40 passing.

Game Details

Alabama 40 • Florida 39

Alabama	3	10	6	14	7	**40**
Florida	7	0	15	11	6	**39**

Date: October 2, 1999

Team Records: Alabama 3–1, Florida 4–0

Scoring Plays:

UA Kemp 37-yard field goal

UF Jackson 73-yard pass from Johnson (Chandler kick)

UA S. Alexander 1-yard rush (Kemp kick)

UA Kemp 22-yard field goal

UF B. Alexander 42-yard interception return (Chandler kick)

UA S. Alexander 47-yard pass from Zow (pass failed)

UF Jackson 8-yard pass from Johnson (Wells pass from Johnson)

UA Carter 14-yard pass from Zow (Kemp kick)

UF Chandler 37-yard field goal

UF Jackson 14-yard pass from Johnson (Carroll rush)

UA S. Alexander 13-yard rush (Kemp kick)

UF Caldwell 6-yard pass from Johnson (kick failed)

UA S. Alexander 25-yard rush (Kemp kick)

It was no surprise that Florida media wondered if Zow, who had suffered a knee injury in high school and wasn't recruited by the Gators, had played with revenge on his mind. "I don't play to get back at somebody," Zow said. "I play for The University of Alabama."

Fans of offense loved watching the game, as Florida edged Bama 449 yards to 447.

At the end of the regular season, Alabama had won the Southeastern Conference Western Division and Florida had won the East. They met in the SEC Championship Game in Atlanta, and most expected the Gators to extract revenge for Bama's upset in the Swamp. Instead, Alabama romped over Florida 34–7.

October 8, 1977

Mad Rush

Wayne Hamilton's Two Big Plays Upend Southern Cal

A routine ploy of former Alabama coach Paul Bryant was to move players up and down the depth chart. The Crimson Tide legend had a knack of knowing how to motivate a player by giving him more playing time or by cutting his snaps. Wayne Hamilton was motivated by the latter.

After starting the first two games of the year, the young defensive end was demoted to second team for the Vanderbilt game. He fought his way back and had a good game against Georgia. But the real test was coming. The Crimson Tide was headed to Los Angeles to take on No. 1 Southern Cal.

As had been the case in previous Alabama games against Southern Cal, the 1977 team was an underdog. Bryant told his players before the game to keep the game close. He said if the teams were within a touchdown of one another at halftime, Alabama would win in the second half. The Tide counted on USC not being familiar with the wishbone offense. Bama quarterback Jeff Rutledge said, "They play different football out here. We were going to beat them with the wishbone."

It didn't look like it was going to be close. Southern Cal took the opening kickoff and marched relentlessly toward the Alabama goal. But USC tailback Charles White was stopped for a loss on a third-and-1 at the Bama 14, and the Trojans had to settle for a field goal.

That was the only score of the first half. In the dressing room, Bryant reminded his team that the game was within a touchdown.

Alabama took the lead in the third quarter when Johnny Davis scored on a two-yard run. Later in the quarter, USC seemed poised to score again with a first-and-goal at the Alabama 2. Two runs up the middle and then a wide sweep failed, and USC settled for another field goal.

Alabama stumbled to its second touchdown. Starting in the third quarter and ending in the fourth quarter, the march included two Alabama fumbles that were blown dead by penalties. Finally, Tony Nathan ran for a touchdown and a 14–6 lead.

Moments later, one of the biggest plays of the game led to a 21–6 Alabama lead. Defensive tackle Curtis McGriff got a hand on a pass by USC quarterback Rob Hertel. Tide defensive end Wayne Hamilton had been blocked to the

Alabama's defense was instrumental in the Tide's upset of No. 1 USC in 1977.

Wayne Hamilton

During his Alabama career, Wayne Hamilton was a second team All-American and first team All-SEC and Academic All-SEC defensive end, a position that would be called an outside linebacker in later football nomenclature. Hamilton missed playing time in both his junior and senior seasons, but was among Bama's leading tacklers all three years (1977–79). Alabama went 34–2 in his three seasons and won three SEC championships and two national titles. His game against Southern Cal was the highlight of his career as he earned numerous national awards as the Player of the Week.

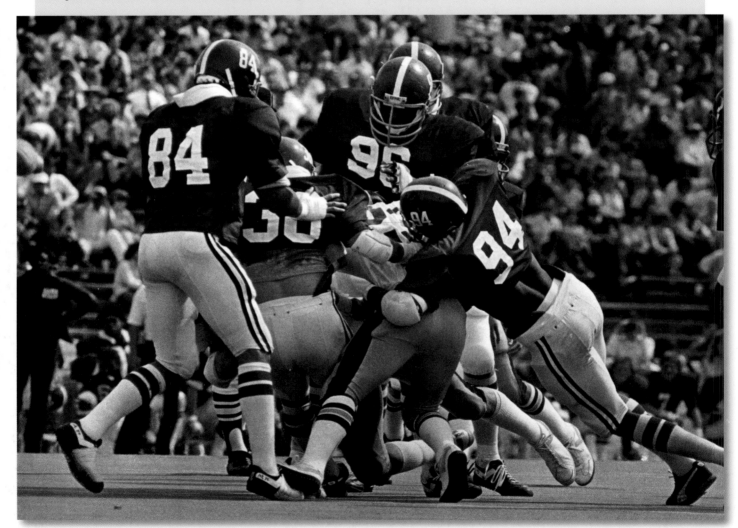

Wayne Hamilton won three SEC titles and two national championships during his three-year Alabama career.

ground, but when the batted ball came to him, he made the interception at the Southern Cal 8. After a motion penalty, Nathan went around right end for the touchdown. After the game, Bryant said, "We had one big play by big Curtis McGriff, which almost makes it worth me putting up with him this long." (McGriff was a sophomore.)

With time and score against them, the Trojans went to the air. Hertel passed for one touchdown and then converted a two-point conversion to pull USC to within 21–14. He finished the game 18-of-30 for 239 yards, a touchdown, and just the one fluke interception. With less than a minute to go, a Hertel pass was knocked down at the line of scrimmage by Tide linebacker Barry Krauss, but Bama cornerback Don McNeal was called for pass interference in the end zone, giving the Trojans a first down at the 1. Lynn Cain ran in for the touchdown, and the Trojans had pulled to within a point of Alabama with 35 seconds to play.

USC coach John Robinson never considered kicking for a tie. The two-point conversion try would determine the outcome.

The Trojans lined up on the left hash marks with wide receivers on each side. As Hertel half-rolled to the right, he was supposed to read the defense and throw to either fullback Mosi Tatupu (who had caught an earlier two-point pass) or flanker Calvin Sweeney.

Hertel began his rollout, but the motivated Hamilton blew off the corner and grabbed Hertel by the legs, pulling him to the ground. There was no whistle and Hertel managed to get an off-balance, off-target pass away. Krauss grabbed it for Alabama, preserving the win.

Alabama had not been surprised by the call. "It was a TB-Go," Hamilton said of the defensive call. "I don't remember who I got around. I just remember it was a huge guy." The "huge guy" was future All-Pro Anthony Munoz, the biggest player in the game at 6'6" and 280 pounds.

Hertel said, "He got in there so fast, he obscured my vision. I couldn't see where to throw and then he had me around my legs."

> **K**ick? God, no, we didn't think of that. I couldn't come into the locker room and look my team in the face if I had gone for a tie. You play to win the game. That's the only way. The kids play too hard out there, and they don't play to tie.
>
> —JOHN ROBINSON, USC COACH

Game Details

Alabama 21 • Southern Cal 20

Alabama	0	0	7	14	**21**
Southern Cal	3	0	3	14	**20**

Date: October 8, 1977
Team Records: Alabama 3–1, Southern Cal 4–0
Scoring Plays:
USC Jordan 32-yard field goal
UA Davis 2-yard rush (Chapman kick)
USC Jordan 23-yard field goal
UA Nathan 1-yard rush (Chapman kick)
UA Nathan 13-yard rush (Chapman kick)
USC Sweeney 10-yard pass from Hertel (Tatupu pass from Hertel)
USC Cain 1-yard rush (pass failed)

Hamilton led all tacklers with 11 (seven primary, four assists) as Alabama ended Southern Cal's 15-game winning streak.

Bryant said, "I would have gone for two points if I'd have been in Robinson's position. The game was tied when it started, and I guess he just didn't want it to end that way."

November 23, 1996

Last Grasp

Kitchens and Riddle Give Stallings Final Win over Auburn

Alabama coach Gene Stallings was a big winner in his seven years as leader of Crimson Tide football. It took external factors—notably his contentious relationship with a new athletics director—to counterbalance the fun and cause him to leave that job with two years remaining on his contract.

An Alabama-Auburn football game absorbs most of the attention in the Heart of Dixie. The rumor of a Stallings resignation didn't diffuse interest in the Crimson Tide against the Tigers. It was an adjunct issue.

In addition to a decision about his future, Stallings had two important ones to make for the game against Auburn. In the previous Alabama game at Mississippi State, a 17–16 loss, quarterback Freddie Kitchens had struggled and place-kicker Jon Brock had missed an extra point. After considering changes, Stallings stuck with his quarterback and kicker. Those would prove to be good decisions.

Another subplot of the game cast Bill "Brother" Oliver playing the role of adversary. A former Tide player and longtime assistant coach under Paul Bryant and then defensive coordinator under Stallings, Oliver had gone over to the dark side. It was his second stint as an Auburn assistant coach, and now he was serving as defensive coordinator under Terry Bowden for the Tigers. Although he was not well known in 1996, Oliver's graduate assistant was Will Muschamp, who would go on to be a famed defensive coordinator at both Auburn and Texas.

Alabama got off to a blistering start, scoring two touchdowns and a field goal on its first three possessions. But before halftime, Alabama's 17–3 first-quarter lead evaporated, primarily because of Crimson Tide mistakes. A long Auburn touchdown pass, an interception returned for a touchdown, and then a field goal set up by an Alabama fumble on the ensuing kickoff gave the Tigers a 20–17 halftime lead.

Auburn added another field goal in the third quarter for a 23–17 lead. Alabama had been its own worst enemy, surrendering three interceptions and two lost fumbles. "Even with the five turnovers, nobody gave up," Kitchens said.

The Bama offense had done almost nothing since the first quarter. With 2:14 to play in the game, Alabama had the ball at its own 26 needing a touchdown and extra point. To the surprise of almost everyone, Alabama started the

Dennis Riddle's six-yard touchdown reception gave Gene Stallings the win in his final game as Alabama head coach against Auburn.

There's pressure at Alabama, but there's nothing wrong with having high expectations and any coach needs to know that going in. Coach Bryant set the standard in the modern era, and it's high. And I was aware of that.

—GENE STALLINGS, ALABAMA COACH

drive in shotgun formation. It was a surprise because Bama had not used the formation during the year.

Offensive coordinator Woody McCorvey said later the Tide had worked on the shotgun "a little" in the week of practice. Jimmy Fuller, who coached the offensive line, suggested the Tide's offensive coordinator "had lost his mind" by going to the shotgun.

The drive didn't start well. Two passes were incomplete before Kitchens hit Shumari Buchanan on a 14-yard gain that stopped the clock with 1:58 left. There was another incompletion and then Kitchens completed a pass to tailback Dennis Riddle for a 16-yard gain to the Auburn 46. Another pass to Riddle left Bama at the Auburn 34 with 1:40 to play.

On the next play, the Tigers were called for pass interference; from the 17, Kitchens scrambled for seven and then completed a pass to Michael Vaughn for a first down at the 6. Kitchens then misfired for Riddle, stopping the clock with 32 seconds to play.

Kitchens looked first for Vaughn when play resumed. "The outside linebacker dropped off to cover me, so when Freddie looked, I wasn't open," Vaughn said. Marcell West seemed to be open, but Kitchens couldn't see him because an Auburn defender blocked his vision.

Riddle was the safety valve, curling out from his halfback position just to the left of Kitchens. As on previous plays in the drive, no Auburn defender picked up Riddle.

Riddle said he had been told to get out of bounds if he couldn't score. When he caught the ball, he made a nice move back to the inside and went in untouched. "All I had to do was run," he said.

Auburn nose tackle Jimmy Brumbaugh said, "When I saw No. 29 [Riddle] run out slowly into the flat, I knew exactly what they were going to do. He's a hard back to cover one-on-one. I knew it was going to be trouble."

And all Brock had to do was kick. Riddle's score had tied the game at 23–23. Brock's third successful extra-point kick was the winning point with 26 seconds to play.

Game Details

Alabama 24 • Auburn 23

Auburn	3	17	3	0	**23**
Alabama	17	0	0	7	**24**

Date: November 23, 1996
Team Records: Alabama 8–2, Auburn 7–3
Scoring Plays:
UA Alexander 63-yard pass from Kitchens (Brock kick)
UA Brock 32-yard field goal
UA Vaughn 7-yard pass from Kitchens (Brock kick)
AU Holmes 34-yard field goal
AU Bailey 57-yard pass from Craig (Holmes kick)
AU Ward 34-yard interception return (Holmes kick)
AU Holmes 33-yard field goal
AU Holmes 34-yard field goal
UA Riddle 6-yard pass from Kitchens (Brock kick)

Birmingham News sportswriter Steve Kirk reported after the game that Oliver, working in the Auburn coaching booth in the press box, had instructed Muschamp to adjust the Auburn coverage. Muschamp's signal was picked up by two defensive backs, but missed by two others.

In the interview room following the game, Stallings made his blockbuster announcement without emotion. "I visited with the players and the coaches, and I told them that there comes a time when you have to pass the torch," Stallings said. "I'm basically the only one left from the old regime. We've got a new president, a new athletics director, a new provost, a new compliance director, a new chairman of the faculty athletics committee. There have been a lot of changes, and sometimes it's best to step aside and let change go on."

Freddie Kitchens

Freddie Kitchens would have been known as the Auburn-killer but for two moments. In the final seconds of the 1995 game in Auburn, Kitchens threw a pass to Curtis Brown in the back of the end zone. It would have been the game-winner. Unfortunately, an official had been injured earlier in the game. With no official in position to see the catch, it was ruled incomplete. In 1997, Alabama was running out the clock with a 17–15 lead, but the Tide fumbled, Auburn recovered, and the Tigers kicked a game-winning field goal. Kitchens was a three-year starter at quarterback and had career passing yardage of 4,668 yards and 30 touchdowns. He ranked third in Alabama history in career attempts, fourth in career passing yards, and fifth in career completions upon his departure. Alabama went 22–13 and he quarterbacked the Tide into three bowl games. At Etowah High School in Attalla, he was a prep All-American and Mr. Football in Alabama. Kitchens played one year of professional football in Italy. He has gone on to an impressive coaching career in college (including under Nick Saban at LSU) and in the NFL.

Quarterback Freddie Kitchens was a three-year starter and led the Tide to three bowl appearances.

October 20, 1973

First and Long Gone

Tide Surprises Tennessee on Game's First Play

Alabama had opened the first five games of 1973 with a simple fullback dive. Crimson Tide quarterback Gary Rutledge said, "We always opened with a dive play just to get recognition. We wanted to see how the corners were going to react, who was going to take the fullback in the triple option, where were the safeties going, and so forth."

Bama was hosting Tennessee at Legion Field in Birmingham in a battle of top-10 teams. Wayne Wheeler, the only split receiver in Alabama's basic wishbone offense, spent most of his practice time as a blocker, but Wheeler could run and catch with the best of them. "I remember that week that we were practicing a play-action pass off that basic dive play," Wheeler said. "I thought since we had started every game by running the dive, it would be interesting if we threw it.

"But I didn't know about it until Gary told me Friday night before the game. He said if the situation was right, we might go for it. The quarterbacks spent a lot of time with Coach Bryant and they knew what was going on."

Alabama had the ball on its 20-yard line to start the game. As almost everyone expected, the Crimson Tide's first-down play looked just like it had in every other game of 1973. Those up in the end-zone stands probably had forgotten the pregame prediction of a young fellow sitting nearby.

"I predict we start the game with a long pass over the middle," the prodigy said. Little did they know that big brother Gary had tipped off little brother Jeff Rutledge—a future star quarterback for the Tide.

Wheeler said, "Our coaches were the best at figuring things out. I'm sure they had scouted Tennessee and they also knew how Tennessee would scout us. I always had the feeling that we had been setting up Tennessee for a few weeks."

Quarterbacks coach Mal Moore said that Bryant thought the play would work. "He did a good job of convincing the players it would work, because they had to sell it to the Tennessee defense," Moore said. "It had to look like a run."

"It was perfect," Rutledge said. "Tennessee had obviously looked at film and knew we always ran a dive play on first down. I don't know why they were so aggressive in going after the fullback, but everybody came flying up... cornerbacks, safeties, everybody."

Gary Rutledge and the Tide caught Tennessee off-guard by passing out of the wishbone on their first play from scrimmage in 1973.

"I faked the handoff to [fullback] Ellis Beck and put the ball on my hip," Rutledge said. "When I looked downfield, it was too good to be true. Wayne was so open I was actually scared. No one was within 15 yards of him. I didn't want to overthrow him and I didn't want to underthrow him so much they could catch him. I underthrew it a little, but it was no problem. Not many people could catch Wayne."

Wheeler said, "When I came off the line of scrimmage, I started smiling. I was running south and all the defensive backs were running north. I blew by the cornerback, there was no safety, and all I had to worry about was Gary being able to get the pass off. When I turned back to look for the ball, I realized it had worked just like we had drawn it up. It was probably the easiest completion we had in our careers."

Wheeler said, "It was the most memorable play in my Alabama career. It's the play that fans still talk about to me. There weren't nearly as many nationally televised games then as there are now, and that was on national television."

Rutledge said, "Later that year I was National Back of the Week and had my picture on the cover of *Sports Illustrated* for my play against LSU, but everyone remembers the start to the Tennessee game."

Bryant had been convinced early in scheming the wishbone that it could be an effective passing offense. "You're trying to get one-on-one coverage in the passing game and you have it every down in the wishbone," he said.

Tennessee coach Bill Battle, who had been a star end on Bryant's 1961 national championship team, said, "The first play was a total shock. We got caught flat-footed. Our guys rolled up to stop the run, and that was it."

Anyone who thought a rout was on was mistaken. Tennessee had the nation's longest winning streak at 11 and the Vols had come to play.

"Tennessee had a tough defense and they had Condredge Holloway at quarterback," Rutledge said. "They fought back. I think we had them 14–0 and then 21–7, but by the end of the third quarter it was 21–21."

Game Details

Alabama 42 • Tennessee 21

Tennessee	7	7	7	0	**21**
Alabama	14	7	0	21	**42**

Date: October 20, 1973
Team Records: Alabama 5–0, Tennessee 5–0
Scoring Plays:
UA Wheeler 80-yard pass from Rutledge (Davis kick)
UA Jackson 8-yard rush (Davis kick)
UT Yarbrough 20-yard pass from Holloway (Townsend kick)
UA Shelby 11-yard pass from Todd (Davis kick)
UT Holloway 6-yard rush (Townsend kick)
UT Gravitt 64-yard pass from Holloway (Townsend kick)
UA Cary 62-yard punt return (Davis kick)
UA Jackson 80-yard rush (Davis kick)
UA Spivey 3-yard rush (Davis kick)

Alabama managed to pull away in the fourth quarter, thanks to a 62-yard punt return for a touchdown by Robin Cary and then a touchdown run by halfback Wilbur Jackson.

Alabama kept the actual time of every play during the game. The opening play of the game took 8.9 seconds. Jackson's winding run took 15.8 seconds. Cary's punt return took 20.9 seconds, the longest of any play of the day.

Alabama was headed to an 11–1 record and the UPI national championship.

> **I** believe Alabama is better than the national championship team I played on in 1961. Coach Bryant has more good players now than he did then.
>
> **—BILL BATTLE, TENNESSEE COACH**

Gary Rutledge

Gary Rutledge was Southeastern Conference Back of the Year as a junior in 1973, then suffered a separated shoulder and saw only limited action through most of 1974. He was named National Back of the Week for his play against LSU in 1973, the Crimson Tide's 500th all-time victory and a game in which Bama clinched the SEC championship. In his 1973 junior season he had 78 rushes for 253 yards and six touchdowns, and completed 33 of 57 passes for 897 yards and eight touchdowns.

Gary Rutledge led Alabama to a national championship during his junior year.

Safety Rashad Johnson picked off three passes and returned one for a touchdown against LSU in a 2008 overtime thriller.
Photo courtesy of Stuart McNair

November 8, 2008

Bayou Backbreaker

Johnson's Interceptions Led Tide to Overtime Win

It's not unusual to see a little blood when two Southeastern Conference football teams go into combat. Ordinarily, though, it's not bad blood. SEC teams have respect for one another and the battles stay between the lines.

Alabama and LSU had no history of animosity, but that changed when Alabama hired the former coach of the Tigers in January 2007. Bama didn't take Nick Saban from LSU; Saban left LSU for the Miami Dolphins of the National Football League in 2005. But two years later, Saban left the Dolphins to become head coach of the Crimson Tide. The move didn't agree with those in Baton Rouge, though, because it was LSU that had brought Saban to the South in the first place. Saban had been head coach at LSU from 2000 through 2004. Before he left, he had restored luster to LSU, leading the Tigers to the 2003 national championship.

LSU had a come-from-behind win over Alabama in Tuscaloosa in Saban's first year, a victory that was part of LSU's 2007 national championship run. But what the Bengal Tigers partisans were really waiting for was Saban's return to Baton Rouge in 2008. There were well-publicized pregame abominations such as a scarecrow-type likeness of Saban being hung in effigy, then burned. There was a semblance of party atmosphere, but an underlying current of menace. When Saban came out for the start of the game, he was escorted by a dozen police officers.

Saban said he ignored the tension. There was more to worry about, notably that Saban knew LSU had good players. After all, he had recruited a number of them. Whether Saban and his players wanted to acknowledge it, there was also the pressure of Alabama being undefeated and ranked No. 1 in the nation. Additionally, the Tide was in position to clinch the SEC Western Division championship.

Twice, Alabama was poised to wrap up the game before a record crowd in Tiger Stadium; both times the Tide made crucial mistakes. With the score tied 21–21 and time winding down in the fourth quarter, Alabama quarterback John Parker Wilson scrambled down the right sideline for an apparent 32-yard touchdown. But hold on. In fact, that's exactly what an official detected—Alabama holding.

Moments later, it seemed the Tide would win in regulation with a field goal. Leigh Tiffin had an excellent record as a place-kicker, and the Tide were set up for a 29-yard field-goal attempt on the final play of the game. But Tiffin kicked low, the attempt was blocked, and Bama and LSU headed to overtime.

Alabama's defensive staff had been paying attention. LSU had been successful with a quarterback rollout to the right; Tigers quarterback Jarrett Lee had completed that pass three times in the second half. LSU, which had possession to begin overtime, faced third-and-6 at the Bama 21. Alabama sent a blitz from the left side and forced Lee into a hurried throw. The pass sailed over the intended receiver's hands and into those of Crimson Tide safety Rashad Johnson.

It was Johnson's third interception of the game. He had returned one of his previous picks 54 yards for a touchdown.

> **I** never got a sense of guys giving in. We were beating ourselves. We had some shots and we missed some opportunities. It was really our first time to come from behind, play the whole game, and win it in overtime. I think it's great for our team.
>
> —JOHN PARKER WILSON, ALABAMA QUARTERBACK

Rashad Johnson

Rashad Johnson was the poster child for those who discount recruiting rankings, frequently cited for going from "no star to all-star." Johnson was a walk-on running back in 2004, when he was redshirted. He played on special teams and as a nickel back as a freshman, became a starting safety in his sophomore season of 2006, then was All–Southeastern Conference in 2007 and 2008. He was a two-time Alabama captain and as a senior was All-America and SEC Defensive Player of the Year. In his final two seasons at Alabama he had 11 interceptions, which he returned for 189 yards and two touchdowns. He caused four fumbles and was in on 217 tackles.

Game Details

Alabama 27 • LSU 21

Alabama	7	7	7	0	6	**27**
LSU	14	0	0	7	0	**21**

Date: November 8, 2008
Team Records: Alabama 9–0, LSU 6–2
Scoring Plays:
UA Wilson 1-yard rush (Tiffin kick)
LSU Byrd 30-yard pass from Lee (David kick)
LSU Scott 30-yard rush (David kick)
UA Johnson 54-yard interception return (Tiffin kick)
UA Coffee 3-yard rush (Tiffin kick)
LSU Scott 1-yard rush (David kick)
UA Wilson 1-yard rush (no PAT attempt)

But his overtime interception was, in the words of Saban, "the biggest play of the game."

When Wilson took the offense onto the field for Bama's overtime possession, Saban said, "Let's take a shot." On first down, Wilson completed a pass to freshman sensation Julio Jones for a 23-yard gain to the LSU 2-yard line. On second down, Wilson bulled in for a 27–21 Alabama win. Saban was a victor in Baton Rouge and Alabama had a 10–0 record.

"Of course, we threw it to Julio," Wilson said. "He made a great play. It was a back-shoulder ball and he made a great adjustment."

Johnson had made the plays to set up the winning score, and he thought the blitz was key. "I saw him roll out," the safety said. "It was a great play for us to blitz him on that side so he couldn't get all the way out and throw the 'out' route like he normally does. He overthrew the receiver."

Johnson had done his homework in preparation for the LSU game. He knew that Lee, a redshirt freshman, had thrown 10 interceptions and that five of them had been returned for touchdowns. "In watching film, I saw some of his pick-sixes and it looked like if we could put pressure on him, we might have some success," Johnson said.

While Johnson was a virtual unknown when he walked on at Alabama, Jones was among the nation's top prospects as a high school senior, ranked by Scout Media as a five-star receiver. He finished the day with seven catches for 128 yards and was Bama's top receiver in his freshman year with 58 catches for 924 yards and four touchdowns.

> **O**ur players overcame a lot of adversity. You've got to keep playing the next play, no matter what happened on the last play. That's what we asked our players to do. We told our defensive players when they went out there for overtime, "You've got to make a play. You've got to get them stopped, and we'll win the game."
>
> —NICK SABAN, ALABAMA COACH

Nick Saban

Nick Saban was named the 27th head coach in University of Alabama football history when he joined the Crimson Tide on January 3, 2007. He came to Bama from the Miami Dolphins. Prior to that he had been a head coach at Toledo (1990), Michigan State (1995–99), and LSU (2000–04). He also served as an assistant coach in both college and the NFL after completing his playing career at Kent State. He led LSU to the national championship and has been National Coach of the Year both at LSU and at Alabama. His second Alabama team was ranked No. 1 in the nation for five weeks in 2008.

Nick Saban took over as Alabama head coach in 2007, four years after winning a national championship at LSU. *Photo courtesy of Stuart McNair*

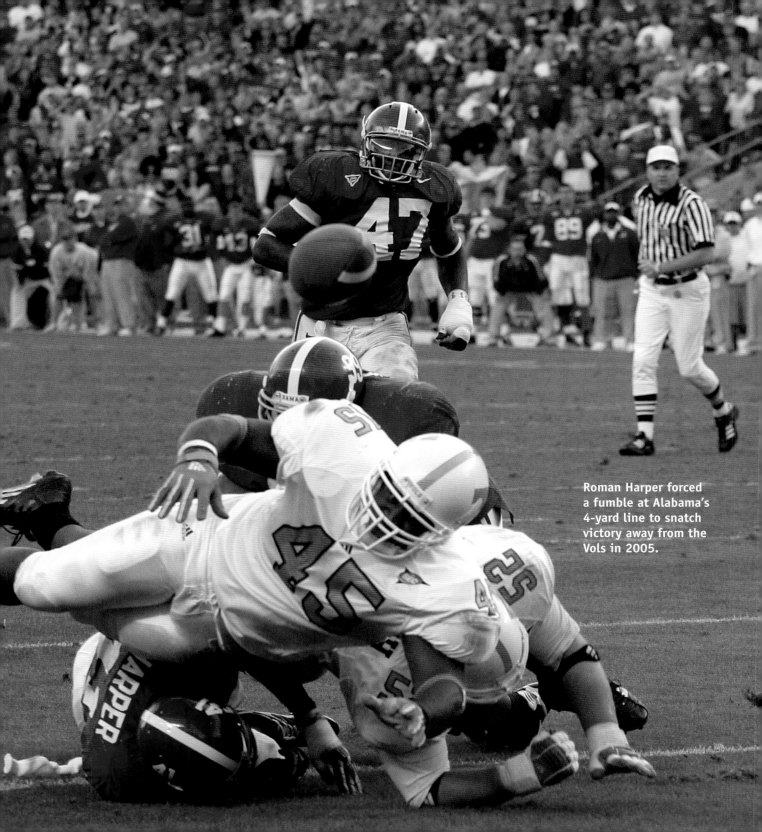

Roman Harper forced a fumble at Alabama's 4-yard line to snatch victory away from the Vols in 2005.

October 22, 2005

Rocky Stop

Roman Harper Saves the Day by Forcing Goal-Line Fumble

The Tennessee band was tuning up for another rendition of its "Rocky Top" theme song in Bryant-Denny Stadium. The Volunteers were marching relentlessly toward the Alabama goal line—and victory. With the score tied 3–3, Tennessee had a first-and-goal at the Alabama 4-yard line with 6:45 to play. It appeared there would be no joy for the home team in a series that had come to be dominated by Tennessee. The Vols of coach Phil Fulmer had won nine of the previous 10 games. On-the-field disappointment had done great damage to Alabama pride; in addition, recent disclosures had shown that Fulmer's undocumented testimony to the NCAA had resulted in unprecedented penalties against the Crimson Tide. Fulmer had vowed to put Alabama out of business. Scholarship cuts had left Alabama football a feeble rival.

Then, on a day of great defense, Roman Harper made the play that staved off almost certain defeat.

Tennessee's luck began to change when senior tailback Gerald Riggs suffered a season-ending broken ankle on his first-down run to the Alabama 4. With victory so close, the Vols began to unravel. A false-start penalty pushed the Vols back to the 9, then they were pushed back farther when Jeremy Clark made a tackle for loss. A second-down play was ruled an illegal pass beyond the line of scrimmage. The penalty is only five yards, but includes a loss of down. On third down, quarterback Rick Clausen completed a screen pass to fullback Cory Anderson, who made a nice run to inside the Alabama 5.

Senior Alabama safety Roman Harper had the angle on Anderson and made the stop short of the goal line. Harper was understandably confused at the roar of the crowd following his hit.

"I thought they had scored," he said.

Harper had no idea that his helmet had hit squarely on the football, knocking it from Anderson's grasp. Moreover, the fumbled ball managed to roll into the end zone, then out of bounds, making it a touchback. Alabama took possession of the football at its 20-yard line.

"I wasn't trying to strip it or anything," Harper said. "I was just trying to stop him from getting into the end zone. My helmet hitting the ball and him fumbling it out of the end zone just happened."

Roman Harper

Roman Harper was a four-year regular (2002–05) and three-year starter for the Crimson Tide and was an All-SEC safety as a senior. He had 38 consecutive starts for Bama. As a sophomore he was in on 114 tackles, joining DeMeco Ryans (126) and Derrick Pope (105) for an Alabama first: three players with more than 100 tackles in the same season. He was a Thorpe Award semifinalist as the nation's best defensive back as a senior. Among Tide defensive backs, he was Alabama's leading tackler three years. He finished his career with a total of 302 tackles including 19 for losses. He had five interceptions and caused five fumbles (recovering three). He also scooped up a loose ball after a blocked field goal at Hawaii and returned it 73 yards for a touchdown.

> **There's fortune and there's misfortune. Sometimes you are lucky and the ball bounces your way. If Roman Harper doesn't make that hit the way he does, the ball doesn't pop out. I'd say we're lucky to have Roman Harper.**
>
> —MIKE SHULA, ALABAMA COACH

Game Details

Alabama 6 • Tennessee 3

Tennessee	0	0	0	3	3
Alabama	0	0	3	3	6

Date: October 22, 2005
Team Records: Alabama 6–0, Tennessee 3–2
Scoring Plays:
UA Christensen 33-yard field goal
UT Wilhoit 32-yard field goal
UA Christensen 34-yard field goal

Now Alabama had 5:08 and 80 yards to go in hopes of getting the victory against Tennessee.

Bama was struggling on offense largely because its heart was watching the game from a hospital bed. Tyrone Prothro had suffered a career-ending injury, a broken leg, two weeks earlier in a 31–3 win over Florida. Prothro had been the Tide's major offensive threat as receiver, runner, and kick-return specialist.

With Brodie Croyle at quarterback, Alabama went to work. Two runs gained almost nothing and the element of surprise was gone. Everyone knew Croyle would be passing, and the Vols called an all-out blitz. Croyle stood in the pocket and delivered his best pass of the day. Wide receiver D.J. Hall, playing with ribs injured a week earlier, had inked reminders of Prothro on his wristbands. Hall said Prothro probably would have made the catch more spectacular, but it couldn't have been more dramatic. Hall made the catch at the Tennessee 35, right in front of Fulmer. The third-and-9 play had gained 44 yards.

Kenneth Darby had a couple of first-down runs, including an 11-yard run to the Tennessee 14 with 1:53 to play. Three runs lost a yard, but those runs ate up the clock and put the ball in the center of the field. Both teams used timeouts. Kicker Jamie Christensen faced his second game-winning opportunity in as many weeks.

Later Christensen would say, "I've done it a thousand times. The only difference is what's at stake. It's pretty much the same routine."

Drew Lane snapped, Matt Miller put the ball down, and Christensen kicked it through for a 34-yard field goal. Alabama

Brodie Croyle connected with D.J. Hall on a 43-yard pass to set up Jamie Christensen's game-winning field goal.

led 6–3 with 13 seconds to play and would hold on for the victory.

Alabama defensive coordinator Joe Kines called Harper's tackle "the defensive play of the century." It marked the 28th consecutive game under Kines the defense had caused a turnover.

Harper would not call it the game-winning play. "It takes a lot of plays to win," he said. "Coach Kines said it perfectly. He told us before the game that when we were born, we were born with something deep inside. And he said, 'When you get your backs to the wall, you've got to dig deep and find that something.' We found it two or three times today."

It was no surprise that Christensen was the Special Teams Player of the Week in the Southeastern Conference for the second consecutive week. But Harper lost the SEC Defensive Player of the Week honor to teammate DeMeco Ryans and his game-high 11 tackles.

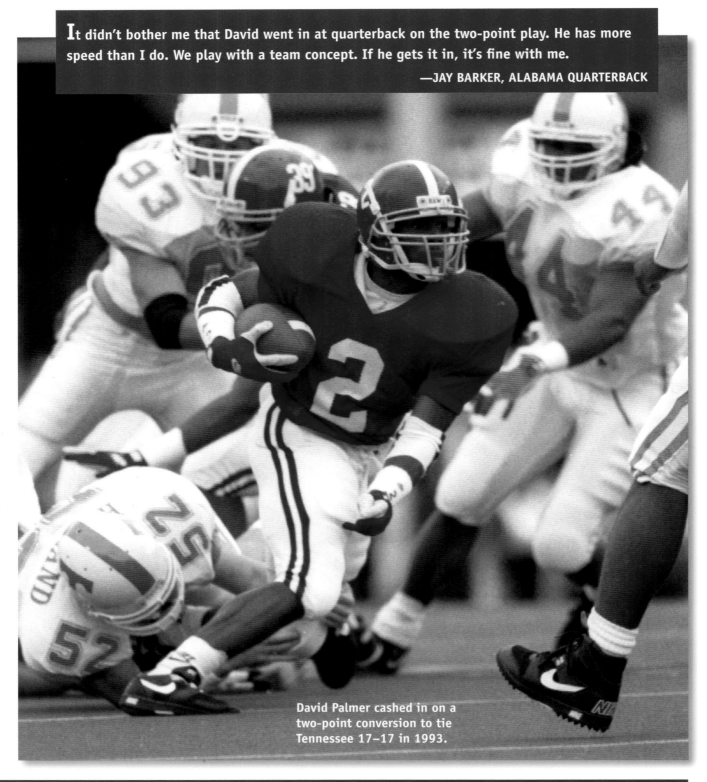

It didn't bother me that David went in at quarterback on the two-point play. He has more speed than I do. We play with a team concept. If he gets it in, it's fine with me.

—JAY BARKER, ALABAMA QUARTERBACK

David Palmer cashed in on a two-point conversion to tie Tennessee 17–17 in 1993.

October 16, 1993

Deuce for Two

Palmer's Two-Point Conversion Ties Vols, Preserves Unbeaten Streak

Legendary Michigan State coach Duffy Daugherty once said, "A tie is like kissing your sister." While that may be true, some kisses are better than others. Alabama's come-from-behind tie against Tennessee probably hurt the Vols as much as a loss. The Crimson Tide, defending national champion and undefeated over its previous 28 games, wasn't happy with the tie, but had to be relieved not to have lost. In 1993 there was no overtime in college football, so 60 minutes decided nothing.

With the game winding down, it appeared the Vols would get a victory, ending Alabama's seven-game winning streak in the series. Tennessee had a 10–9 lead going to the fourth quarter when Vols tailback Charlie Garner went 73 yards for a touchdown to make it 17–9.

The Tide's final drive started with 1:44 to play and Bama backed up on its 17-yard line. As quarterback Jay Barker remembers, "I said, 'Guys, give me time, and we'll take it down and score.' I could tell they had confidence."

Barker delivered. The junior quarterback got it going with a 12-yard pass to fullback Taurus Turner. Then Barker went to David Palmer. Palmer, the diminutive wide receiver/kick returner/running back/quarterback known as the Deuce, managed to get open for receptions of 15 yards, 22 yards, and seven yards on the next three plays. Barker had to scramble and then passed to Kevin Lee for a nine-yard gain and a first down at the Tennessee 18-yard line.

Barker was incomplete on the next three passes. He had called every play in the drive, but quarterbacks coach Mal Moore came up with the fourth-down call. With 30 seconds to play, wide receiver Kevin Lee went on a curl route. Barker hit him, and Lee fought his way to the 1-yard line.

Stallings wasn't taking any chances. He told Barker to sneak it in, and the quarterback took it in for the touchdown with 21 seconds to play.

"We came back and showed a lot of character," Stallings said. "We went the length of the field with no timeouts. We made plays when we had to. That says something about the players."

Barker had completed six of nine passes for 82 yards on the drive. Barker would be the ABC Player of the Game for Alabama as he completed 22 of 40 passes for 312 yards.

As for the final drive, Palmer said, "They loosened the defense on us, so they wouldn't give up the big play. Because of that, we shortened our pass routes. We knew we had to score. We just dug deep to score the touchdown."

But Alabama was not through. The touchdown pulled the Tide to within two points at 17–15. Tennessee coach Phil Fulmer said, "We had seen Palmer at quarterback, so we called a timeout. I thought we were prepared to stop the perimeter play."

That timeout may have worked to Alabama's benefit.

"Coach Stallings recommended we put David in for the two-point run," Moore said. "That was our 'go-for-two' play and we had worked on it in practice, but not with David at quarterback."

David Palmer's three receptions on the final drive put the Tide in position for the game-tying touchdown and two-point conversion.

The Tie of 1965

Before college football devised a tiebreaking overtime system in 1996, Alabama and Tennessee had played to a tie seven times. Prior to this game in 1993, the last tie in the Alabama-Tennessee series had been in 1965, also at Legion Field in Birmingham. It was unusual, to say the least. Alabama had won the national championship in 1964 and would go on to win it again in 1965, despite a couple of blemishes. One of those was the tie with Tennessee. Alabama dominated the game with 22 first downs to Tennessee's 10 and 361 yards to 195 for the Vols, but the Crimson Tide was prone to mistakes. Three lost fumbles kept Tennessee in the game. But Bama seemed poised to win in the final moments. Sophomore Kenny Stabler, a backup quarterback to Steve Sloan, was sent into the game ostensibly as holder for a David Ray field goal on third down. It was a fake, though, and Stabler made a long run to the Tennessee 2-yard line. Thinking he had made a first down, Stabler threw the ball out of bounds to stop the clock. Unfortunately for Alabama, it was fourth down. The ball went over to Tennessee and the Vols ended a four-game losing streak to Bama with the tie. Other Alabama-Tennessee ties occurred in the first game in the series in 1901 (6–6) in Birmingham; in 1936 (0–0) in Birmingham; in 1944 (0–0) in Knoxville; in 1949 (7–7) in Birmingham; and in 1953 (0–0) in Birmingham.

Palmer was at quarterback with tailback Sherman Williams and fullbacks Taurus Turner and Marcus Moring behind him. Palmer took the snap and everyone ran to the right side. Palmer got key blocks from walk-on Moring and right tackle Roosevelt Patterson and threaded his way into the end zone for the tying conversion.

An obviously disappointed Fulmer said, "It was a great football game. It had some great plays, and it had two outstanding teams going at each other's throat. We came into Birmingham to play the defending national champions, and they had to come back and tie us."

The tie focused attention on college football not having an overtime period. Stallings said, "I would have liked it. We would have had the momentum going into an overtime."

The Vols' quarterback, Heath Shuler, agreed. "This one falls into the category of a bitter memory," Shuler said. "A great game is one you win. There should be a tiebreaker. Give each team the ball once, or have four minutes to play. It makes no sense to have a tie."

Fulmer disagreed. "I don't know if my heart could take it any longer," he said.

Game Details

Alabama 17 • Tennessee 17

Tennessee	7	0	3	7	**17**
Alabama	3	6	0	8	**17**

Date: October 16, 1993

Team Records: Alabama 5–0, Tennessee 5–1

Scoring Plays:

UA Proctor 22-yard field goal

UT Faulkner 25-yard pass from Shuler (Becksvoort kick)

UA Proctor 47-yard field goal

UA Proctor 30-yard field goal

UT Becksvoort 34-yard field goal

UT Garner 73-yard rush (Becksvoort kick)

UA Barker 1-yard rush (Palmer rush)

Truly
Special

November 30, 1985

The Kick

Van Tiffin's Record Field Goal Lifts Tide Over Auburn

Van Tiffin was doing the math. The easy part was that Alabama trailed Auburn by one point. The time could be calculated in seconds, and there weren't many of those. Tiffin, Alabama's place-kicker, was watching the yards.

"I thought we had to get to at least the Auburn 37, maybe 36," Tiffin said.

Alabama was out of timeouts. Crimson Tide quarterback Mike Shula dropped back and threw a perfect strike to split end Greg Richardson for 19 yards. He had a defender hanging onto him, but Richardson, all 5'9" and 166 pounds of him, strained and reached the out-of-bounds line right in front of Auburn coach Pat Dye.

Richardson had made it to the Auburn 35 and stopped the clock with six seconds to play.

"Every kicker would say that the situation that came to me was a dream come true, because a kicker always dreams of making the winning field goal in the last second of a big game," Tiffin said. "But when you're standing on the sideline and see the possibility of it coming down to you, you have second thoughts about it."

Auburn was also out of timeouts in a game that had turned helter-skelter in the fourth quarter. "Everything was just rush-rush-rush, and that's the way I wanted it," Tiffin said. "I didn't want to have to think about it. I didn't really pay a lot of attention to how much time was left. I just tried to think about the kick. I put the tee down on the 42-yard line. I didn't worry about the wind. It was in my face a little. No one said anything to me, and I think that was a good thing, too. I just wanted to think about the kick."

Suddenly, there was no more time to think. "Line set. Snap," came the call from holder Larry Abney.

"I was expecting more of a delay," Tiffin said. "The snap from Butch Lewis was on the money and Larry's hold was perfect, although he had it down quicker than I expected. I was aware of Kevin Porter, Auburn's defensive end, coming from my left. He was offside. He dove by me, so I knew he wasn't going to block it. If he hadn't been offside, he might have gotten it, but he was early. I got the kick off a little low and was afraid it might get blocked.

"Kicking is a lot like hitting a golf ball or a baseball. When you don't feel anything, you know you've hit it good. And that's the way it was. I can just remember getting back and kicking it, not feeling it, and looking up and there it was, going right down the middle of the uprights. That's the best place. Then everybody went wild."

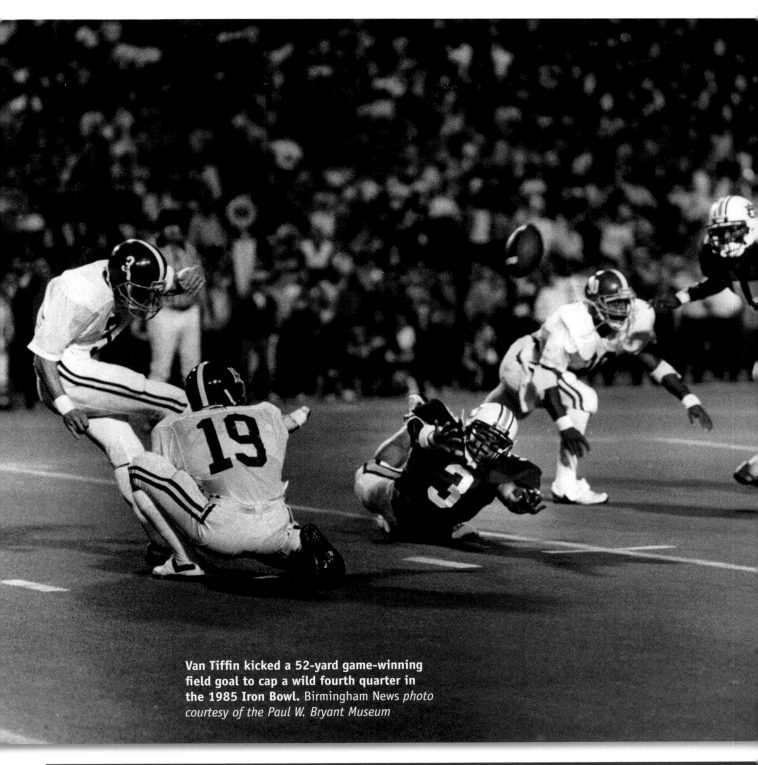

Van Tiffin kicked a 52-yard game-winning field goal to cap a wild fourth quarter in the 1985 Iron Bowl. Birmingham News *photo courtesy of the Paul W. Bryant Museum*

Van Tiffin

Van Tiffin was an All-American in 1986. He was voted to the Alabama Team of the Decade for the 1980s by readers of 'BAMA Magazine and was selected to the Alabama Team of the Century. He holds the NCAA record for best extra-point percentage for a career (135 of 135 for 100 percent). In addition to his game-winning kick against Auburn in 1985, Tiffin also had a game-winning field goal against the Tigers a year earlier. He also kicked the longest field goal in Alabama history, a 57-yarder against Texas A&M. He made 59 of 88 field goals and scored 312 points before moving on to the NFL and kicking for the Miami Dolphins and Tampa Bay Buccaneers. His son Leigh followed him as an Alabama place-kicker.

Van Tiffin was a perfect 135-for-135 kicking extra points during his Tide career.

Wild was the operative word for a fourth quarter that featured four lead changes. Alabama had a 16–10 lead, but Auburn halfback Bo Jackson scored to give Auburn its first lead of the game at 17–16. One minute later, Bama freshman tailback Gene Jelks went 74 yards for a score and the Tide was back in front 22–17. Reggie Ware's one-yard run gave the Tigers a 23–22 lead with 57 seconds to play and set up the heroic Alabama comeback capped off by Tiffin's 52-yard field goal.

The 50th Alabama-Auburn game was one not likely to be forgotten in the next 50 years.

Jelks, not Heisman Trophy winner Jackson, was the game's leading rusher. Jelks had 18 carries for 192 yards, Jackson 31 rushes for 142 yards.

Shula said, "I've always bragged about being the first one to reach Van after the field goal. I really wasn't first, but I was close. I remember coming off the field after Greg had gotten out of bounds to stop the clock and thinking we had done our job.

"There was never any doubt in my mind that Van would make the kick. You never thought about a miss when Van was kicking."

Bama defensive tackle Larry Roberts said he couldn't watch. "I closed my eyes," he confessed. "I knew Van could make it, but I just couldn't watch. I heard all the fans screaming, but I didn't know if they were Auburn fans screaming because we had missed or Alabama fans screaming because he had made it. Then everybody around me started running out on the field and hollering. I knew it was good and opened my eyes and ran."

Tiffin enjoyed a kicker's dream, but was admittedly uncomfortable about the attention—particularly the ride off the field on the shoulders of his ecstatic teammates. "I was embarrassed," he said. "I was uncomfortable, because I'm a shy person. I would rather they had just let me go to the dressing room. But I also appreciated what they did. It gives you a good feeling when your teammates want to do something like that."

> **T**hat may be the most exciting fourth quarter of offense I have ever seen.
>
> —KEITH JACKSON, ABC BROADCASTER

Game Details

Alabama 25 • Auburn 23

Alabama	10	6	0	9	**25**
Auburn	0	10	0	13	**23**

Date: November 30, 1985
Team Records: Alabama 7–2–1, Auburn 8–2
Scoring Plays:
UA Turner 1-yard rush (Tiffin kick)
UA Tiffin 26-yard field goal
UA Tiffin 32-yard field goal
AU Jackson 7-yard rush (Johnson kick)
UA Tiffin 42-yard field goal
AU Johnson 49-yard field goal
AU Jackson 1-yard rush (Johnson kick)
UA Jelks 74-yard rush (pass failed)
AU Ware 1-yard rush (pass failed)
UA Tiffin 52-yard field goal

> **W**e asked the players to do a lot of things, and they responded with a great attitude. There is a oneness on this team like I knew as a player at Alabama.
>
> —RAY PERKINS, ALABAMA COACH

November 12, 1960

"It Was Digger!"

O'Dell's Last-Second Kick Beats Georgia Tech

Alabama owes its victory over Georgia Tech in 1960 to an unlikely hero: a backup place-kicker. But before he put his name in the Bama record book, a series of mistakes and miscues had left the Tide in a 15–0 halftime hole.

"We had complicated calls," said Alabama quarterback Bobby Skelton. "They used an old mimeograph machine and ran off a few dozen copies of all our plays. They had those plays on a hook and they'd snatch one off and send it in with the halfback. I'd get it, read it, call it out in the huddle, and then I'd stuff the paper into my pants because I didn't want the opponent to find those plays."

In the second half, Alabama got back in the game on a Leon Fuller touchdown run and a Skelton pass to Norbie Ronsonet. A two-point conversion attempt failed after the first touchdown. Richard "Digger" O'Dell, the backup place-kicker, made his first career point with an extra point after the second touchdown to cut the Tech lead to 15–13. O'Dell was an offensive tackle and defensive end, but when regular kicker Tommy Brooker was injured, O'Dell moved up to place-kicker. He had kicked in high school and practiced with Brooker each day.

Late in the game Skelton received a play. "I ran the play and I nearly got killed and I fumbled the ball," Skelton said. "When I got up, I saw [fellow quarterback Pat] Trammell coming in."

With Trammell coming in, Skelton headed to the sideline. "In those days, when you came off the field, you went directly to Coach Bryant," Skelton said. "When I got to him, he told me to sit my ass on the bench and that I'd never play another down for Alabama."

Later in the fourth quarter, Trammell was injured and Skelton was called back into service.

"I went running out there," Skelton said. "Coach Bryant was a few feet on the field and I went up to him. He put his arm around me. I was 5'11" and he was nine feet tall. I was expecting him to give me some real knowledge. He said, 'I'm going to give your little ass one more chance.' We were backed up and he didn't even give me a play."

Alabama had the ball at its 20 with 3:21 to play. Twice in the drive Bama had to go on fourth down, making one first down on a Fuller run and another on a Skelton pass to Ronsonet. With the clock ticking under 30 seconds, Skelton completed a 26-yard pass to Butch Wilson to put Bama at the Georgia Tech 8.

Backup kicker Richard "Digger" O'Dell hits the game-winning field goal for Bama against Georgia Tech in 1960.

Richard O'Dell

Richard O'Dell was a tackle on offense, an end on defense, and the kickoff man for Alabama in 1959, 1960, and 1962. He missed the 1961 national championship season for disciplinary reasons, but returned for the 1962 season when Alabama lost only one game—to Georgia Tech by a score of 7–6 at Grant Field in Atlanta. Alabama did not attempt to kick the extra point against Tech, going for two. The field goal O'Dell kicked against Georgia Tech in 1960 was the only one he kicked in his Alabama career. He never tried another field goal or extra-point kick after the 1960 Georgia Tech game.

Richard O'Dell's kick in 1960 made him an Alabama hero.

Skelton said he waited as O'Dell rushed in from the sideline.

"If Tommy had been able to kick, he would have," O'Dell said. "I had missed two field goals the week before, the only ones I had ever tried, then had made an extra point after a touchdown against Tech."

Skelton was the holder. "Digger called me Rob, and he said, 'Okay, Rob. Give me a good hold and lean 'er back a tad.' Just as calm as you'd ever hear," Skelton said.

The injured Brooker had a clear view from the sideline. He said, "I was watching the ball go over the bar, and as it did I saw the clock go to zero, zero, zero."

"Everyone said the kick looked like a wounded duck, but it wasn't. He didn't put spin on the ball, but he kicked it hard and straight and it went over the crossbar," Skelton said.

O'Dell wore No. 87 and Brooker No. 81. In the Alabama radio broadcast booth, play-by-play man Maury Farrell gave credit for the kick to Brooker. Earlier in the game when Trammell had been injured, Farrell had said, "There's the final nail in Alabama's coffin."

After the game, Phil Cutchin, the assistant coach who sent in plays, asked Skelton why he had run the play that got him pulled from the game.

"I reached into my pants and started pulling out all those paper wads," Skelton said. "Finally I found the play that had been sent in and showed it to Coach Cutchin. He took it, and then turned it over. There was another play written on the back."

A crowd of several hundred met the two team planes at Tuscaloosa Airport that night.

Game Details

Alabama 16 • Georgia Tech 15

Alabama	0	0	6	10	**16**
Georgia Tech	6	9	0	0	**15**

Date: November 12, 1960
Team Records: Alabama 5–1–1, Georgia Tech 5–3
Scoring Plays:
GT Nail 8-yard rush (kick failed)
GT Wells 47-yard field goal
GT Gann 3-yard rush (kick failed)
UA Fuller 1-yard rush (pass failed)
UA Ronsonet 8-yard pass from Skelton (O'Dell kick)
UA O'Dell 24-yard field goal

"I came off the plane and all these girls started kissing me," Brooker said. "I looked over and saw Digger kind of sneaking away. I started yelling, 'It was Digger!'"

On Sunday O'Dell went to his hometown of Lincoln to see his girlfriend (later his wife). "The only thing she knew about the game was what she had heard on the radio," O'Dell said. "She told me she sure was glad it had been Tommy instead of me that had to try the kick because I might have missed it."

I guess you could say they won the first half and we won the second. I believe I prefer the second. There were a lot of big plays in the second half and we could not have won without every one of them. I'd say we were lucky, too. Just one little slip in that last push and the game was over for us.

—PAUL BRYANT, ALABAMA COACH

Philip Doyle's game-winning field goal against Tennessee was set up by Stacy Harrison's blocked kick.

October 20, 1990

Using His Head

Harrison's Blocked Field Goal Leads to Philip Doyle's Game Winner at Tennessee

Alabama coach Gene Stallings had a knack for preparing his place-kickers for pressure. One day in practice a kicker working under the close eye of Stallings said, "Coach, it makes me nervous to have you watch."

Stallings said, "Son, I hate to break this to you, but I plan to be at every game."

Stallings didn't have to worry about Philip Doyle's nerves. What Stallings had to worry about was his team finding a way to win.

After winning the 1989 Southeastern Conference championship, Alabama had opened the 1990 season with three straight losses and some were having doubts about Stallings, Bama's new head coach. The Crimson Tide, having rebounded with wins over lightweights Southwestern Louisiana and Vanderbilt, was in Knoxville to take on undefeated, third-ranked Tennessee, which was averaging more than 42 points per game.

The defense had done its job, but with 1:35 to play and the score tied 6–6, the Vols were at the Alabama 33. Tennessee place-kicker Greg Burke was lined up for a 50-yard field-goal attempt. He had connected from 51 earlier.

Alabama put 11 men on the line. "It was a desperation block," Alabama junior safety Stacy Harrison said. "I was lined up next to George Teague and we were shooting the same gap. The blocker picked up George and no one touched me. I got a good jump on the snap and was totally free."

Harrison stretched out, hoping to block the ball with his hands or arms. He can still see the ball coming off the toe of the Tennessee kicker. "The ball didn't get up," he said. "It hit me right in the facemask. *Thump.* The ball bounced back our way. I was thinking, *Pick it up and score*, but I never got to it. It seemed like it had gone 50 yards, but it was 30."

That 30-yard "gain" occurred because the ball ricocheted so hard off Harrison's helmet. It matched Bama's longest offensive play of the day, a Gary Hollingsworth pass to tight end Steve Busky.

"Every year on the week of the third Saturday in October, I see that game replayed on one of the classic sports channels," Harrison said. "That play was a defining moment in my career. Recently I ran into Chuck Smith, who played for Tennessee and went on to play for Atlanta in the NFL. He told me I ruined their season."

Harrison understands why his block would be remembered. The overall performance of the defense that day, however, is what he recalls most. Before the game, secondary coach Bill Oliver told the defensive backs, "Someone in this group is going to make a play that's going to change our season."

"A lot of people would say that my play did it," Harrison said. "But Coach Oliver told me later that he would always remember an open-field tackle I made on second down. If I don't make the tackle, it's a touchdown. And on third down, Efrum Thomas made a great play to stop a screen pass for a two-yard loss. Antonio Langham and George Teague had interceptions; Mark McMillian and Lorenzo Ward had big plays. It was a team win.

"We had been adjusting to a new coaching staff, new ways. I thought our defense was defined by that game. We lost to Penn State the next week and lost our bowl game, but I think we won 38 of the next 42."

When Harrison blocked the Tennessee field-goal try, it meant Alabama wasn't going to lose. But the game still wasn't won. That would come four plays later. The ball was at the Tennessee 37 with just over a minute to play.

Prior to the final possession, Stallings told Bama quarterbacks coach Mal Moore to make sure that the offense didn't lose the game, and the Tide played conservatively.

"I wasn't going to be passing," Hollingsworth said. "We knew with Philip kicking that we didn't have to move it far." Bama would gain seven yards in three plays.

In the first quarter, the senior had missed a 36-yard attempt. In the second quarter, he had made a 30-yarder, and in the third quarter he had been good from 26 yards.

"My concern was that we protect Philip," Stallings said. "I thought if we gave him a chance, he'd probably make the kick. He likes pressure."

There had to be a good snap, and Matthew Pine delivered that. There had to be a good hold, and Jeff Wall got it down perfectly on the 37-yard line. Doyle knew he had made good contact with the ball, but he didn't get to see anything. A Tennessee defender trying to block the field-goal attempt had been offside and then leveled Doyle.

"For a second I thought the kick had been blocked," Doyle said.

He also said he wished that he had been able to see it.

Alabama faithful saw it. It was perfect, and Alabama had won 9–6.

The referee had thrown a flag on the play, but there was no reason to discuss the penalty against Tennessee. Special teams captain Doyle had been swarmed by his teammates, including the man who made Doyle's heroics possible, Stacy Harrison.

Game Details

Alabama 9 • Tennessee 6

Alabama	0	3	3	3	9
Tennessee	0	0	3	3	6

Date: October 20, 1990

Team Records: Alabama 2–3, Tennessee 4–0–2

Scoring Plays:

UA Doyle 30-yard field goal
UT Burke 20-yard field goal
UA Doyle 26-yard field goal
UT Burke 51-yard field goal
UA Doyle 47-yard field goal

It was a desperation situation where we were rushing everybody and we just happened to get one through. You can call it a break, but I call it a good play. I'll never forget it.

—GENE STALLINGS, ALABAMA COACH

Stacy Harrison

Stacy Harrison was a two-year starter (1990–91) at strong safety for Alabama and was a first-team All–Southeastern Conference selection his senior year. As a senior he was Bama's fifth-leading tackler with 52 stops and three interceptions. As a junior he started every game and had 47 tackles and two interceptions. He also had 10 passes broken up that season and recovered two fumbles. Harrison had been one of the South's top prospects coming out of Mays High School in Atlanta. After being redshirted in 1987, he was a backup to strong safety John Mangum on defense, but made his mark on special teams. In 1989 he continued to perform well on kicking teams, but was again a backup safety, that year to Charles Gardner. When he got his chance to start as a junior he made the most of it, starting every game his final two seasons. After a brief fling with pro football, Stacy and former Tide and NFL star Derrick Thomas went into business. After Thomas' death from injuries in an automobile accident, Harrison returned to his hometown of Atlanta to continue his business career.

Stacy Harrison was a first-team All-SEC performer as a senior.

November 26, 1964

Runback

Ray Ogden's 107-Yard Kickoff Return Beats Auburn

An enduring legend of Alabama football is that Ray Ogden returned a kickoff 107 yards to help beat Auburn in 1964. Legendary New York Yankees manager Casey Stengel was wont to conclude a story with "You can look it up." Looking up Ogden's statistics shows a 100-yard kickoff return against the Tigers. But anyone who saw it knows Ogden caught the kickoff while standing close to the back line of the end zone.

It's no mystery why the kickoff return is listed as 100 yards. As far as the college rule of statistics is concerned, the runback started when Ogden left the end zone.

The big mystery is why he tried to do it in the first place.

Alabama was trailing Auburn 7–6 as the second half started. Alabama coach Paul Bryant likely would have disapproved of taking the ball out from deep in the end zone. But when it was over, everyone in crimson could smile. Alabama

had beaten Auburn, gone 10–0 on the season, and would be national champion.

"It wasn't my decision," Bryant said. "When a ball goes deep like that, one of the other deep backs is supposed to check the kick coverage and tell the receiver what to do. I don't know which of our boys advised Raymond, but it was good advice. And Raymond took it, didn't he?"

Bryant pointed out that Alabama had defeated Auburn in 1962 in part because Butch Wilson returned a kickoff 92 yards against the Tigers, but that was a 38–0 Bama victory.

In 1964, Alabama won the game by one touchdown, so obviously the Ogden kickoff return was important for the points. More than that, the kickoff changed momentum. The underdog Auburn team had taken the fight to Alabama through the first 30 minutes.

Ben McDavid kicked off for Auburn to start the second half and Ogden juggled the ball briefly before pulling it in. There was no hesitation on the part of Larry "Dink" Wall, who directed

Ray Ogden returned the second-half kickoff for an unofficial 107 yards and an Alabama touchdown against Auburn in 1964.

Game Details

Alabama 21 • Auburn 14

Auburn	0	7	0	7	**14**
Alabama	6	0	8	7	**21**

Date: November 26, 1964

Team Records: Alabama 9–0, Auburn 6–3

Scoring Plays:

UA Bowman fumble recovery in end zone (kick failed)

AU Frederickson 3-yard rush (Lewis kick)

UA Ogden 100-yard kickoff return (Sloan rush)

UA Perkins 23-yard pass from Namath (Ray kick)

AU Sidle 16-yard pass from Bryan (Lewis kick)

Ogden to run it out, and no hesitation on the part of Ogden, either.

Ogden followed Wall up the middle of the field, got good blocks that opened up an alley, cut toward the right sideline, and then straightened and outraced the final defender to the end zone.

Gary White, who was an Alabama manager, football scout, and later Bama athletics administrator, described Ogden as not having great starting speed, "but once those long legs get going, he covers a lot of ground in a hurry." It's unlikely the kickoff return took 15 seconds, but that's what ticked off the Legion Field clock.

Ogden said, "One man had a pretty good shot at me, but somebody took him out. The blocking was perfect. I don't know when I was clear. I was just hoping nobody was going to catch me. All I could think of was running the other way."

Ogden became the third Alabama player in history to return a kickoff 100 yards for a touchdown and the first player to do it in an Alabama-Auburn game.

After an Auburn fumble in the fourth quarter, Bama's Steve Bowman ripped up the middle for 52 yards. Moments later, Alabama quarterback Joe Namath completed a 23-yard touchdown pass to Ray Perkins to wrap up the victory. Auburn would get one final late touchdown.

Alabama played two quarterbacks in the win over Auburn, Steve Sloan and Joe Namath. Namath had been hobbled for

Ray Ogden

In his three-year (1962–64) Crimson Tide career, Ray Ogden was listed as a right halfback, which was the equivalent of flanker. He was huge for the day, 6'5" and 215 pounds. Ogden, an outstanding blocker, had relatively modest statistics until his senior season. In his first two years he had 43 rushes for 250 yards and seven pass receptions for 72 yards. As a senior he had five runs for 33 yards and 18 pass receptions for 254 yards and returned 10 kickoffs for 334 yards. His kickoff return against Auburn was the only touchdown he scored in his Alabama career. Ogden was drafted in the third round of the 1965 NFL Draft by the St. Louis Cardinals. St. Louis had drafted Joe Namath in the first round, but Namath elected to sign with the rival AFL team, the New York Jets. Ogden was a receiver for two years for the Cardinals, one year for the New Orleans Saints, two years for the Atlanta Falcons, and three years for the Chicago Bears. He earned at least one more paycheck for football play when he played the part of Schmidt in the 1974 Burt Reynolds football movie, *The Longest Yard*.

much of the year with a knee injury and Sloan suffered a knee injury during the game. For that reason, Bryant pulled halfback Wayne Trimble from the game in the third quarter. Trimble was the third quarterback and Bryant wanted to make sure he had one who was healthy.

Alabama was ranked second in the nation as the final week of college football games was being played. Bryant lobbied for No. 1 votes. He said, "We think we are No. 1 because we came from behind in four big games [Florida, Mississippi State, LSU, and Auburn] to win. And if you'll check the schedules of other teams in the top 10, you'll find that we played the toughest schedule of any team that is nationally ranked. No one can say how good we are, because we've never had everybody healthy at once."

Notre Dame was ranked No. 1, but when the Irish lost to Southern Cal, Alabama was the nation's only undefeated team and won the national championship. The Tide would finish the season in the Orange Bowl against Texas.

Since the early 1960s, Alabama has thoroughly dominated football opponents in the Southeastern Conference. But it wasn't until 1964 that the Tide went ahead of Tennessee for best winning percentage in SEC history. The 1964 win against Auburn tied that series record at 14–14–1.

Ray Perkins and Joe Namath connected for a 23-yard touchdown pass in the fourth quarter to seal the victory.

David Palmer returned a punt for a touchdown and caught a pass for another score in the 1991 Blockbuster Bowl.

December 28, 1991

Back at You

Punt Return Starts Tide on Way to Bowl Win over Colorado

Alabama coach Gene Stallings didn't agree with the assessment that the Tide's 30–25 win over Colorado in the 1991 Blockbuster Bowl in Miami was a "weird game." "It's not weird when you win," Stallings said. "It's weird when you lose. But there were some weird plays."

Colorado was the defending national champion, having won the title in 1990. The Buffaloes had been able to win the national championship in the Orange Bowl the year before in part because a punt return for a touchdown by Notre Dame's famed Rocket Ismail was wiped out by a clipping penalty.

Many in south Florida suspected that the 1992 national championship trophy would be delivered to the nearby Miami Hurricanes. Instead, spectators in Joe Robbie Stadium at the end of 1991 were watching many of the players who would be responsible for Bama winning the 1992 crown.

One of the most important Alabama players was one of the smallest—freshman flanker David Palmer. In his first year with the Crimson Tide, Palmer set the Bama record for most punts returned for touchdowns in a season (three) and most punt-return yards in a season (386).

Among them was a 90-yard punt return for a touchdown against LSU.

It was a game of young players. Alabama was the youngest team in the nation's top 25 with 25 freshmen or sophomores at the one and two spots in the depth chart. Colorado was second with 24.

Surely Colorado's scouting report included Palmer as a punt-return threat. Nevertheless, when the Buffaloes were unable to move on their second possession, they punted to Palmer. Colorado punter Mitch Berger, then a sophomore, was a good one. He went on to a long NFL career, including winning a Super Bowl ring with the Pittsburgh Steelers.

Palmer said later that Alabama had attempted to block the punt, but that the Tide rush men quickly turned to blockers. "I just cut it up and followed my blockers in," he said.

Palmer took the punt at the Alabama 48. He gave a slight hesitation, then burst between four potential Colorado tacklers. He dashed to the right side, then cut upfield where a crimson escort of Andre Royal, Eric Washington, Craig Harris, and Antonio Langham led him into the end zone. Langham took out Berger, the final Colorado player with a chance to get in Palmer's way.

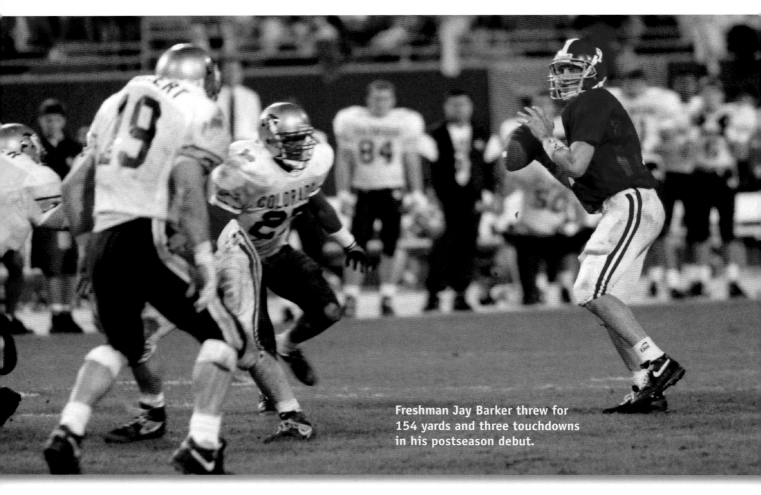

Freshman Jay Barker threw for 154 yards and three touchdowns in his postseason debut.

Colorado coverage men grasping for Palmer and coming up empty-handed brought back memories of something Stallings had said. He told of going to watch Palmer as a high school quarterback. A friend asked him how Palmer, a 5'9", 160-pound quarterback, held up to contact. "I don't know," Stallings said. "I've never seen him get hit."

Palmer's 52-yard punt return was the first postseason punt-return touchdown since Cecil "Hootie" Ingram took one back 80 yards against Syracuse in the 1953 Orange Bowl.

Palmer had given Bama a 7–0 lead, but the game was far from over and neither was Palmer's day. He would add a touchdown on a five-yard diving pass reception from Jay

Barker in the fourth quarter to provide Bama with a 30–25 victory.

Barker, a freshman, was selected to start the game at quarterback. Danny Woodson, a senior, had started the first eight games of the season, but had been suspended for the final three regular-season games. Barker completed 12 of 16 passes for 154 yards and three touchdowns.

Other than the Palmer punt return, Alabama's first half was not a good one. The Tide gave up a blocked punt that led to a Colorado touchdown and also allowed a safety. Even a good play, Mark McMillian's interception and return to the Colorado 1, was bittersweet as the Tide offense couldn't grind out a touchdown and had to settle for a field goal. In the final minute of the half Bama lost a

David Palmer

David Palmer was MVP of the Blockbuster Bowl his freshman year, a key member of Alabama's undefeated national championship team in 1992, and an All-American his junior year in 1993. As a junior he set Alabama records for receiving yards (1,000) in a season, receptions (61) in a season, and receiving yards (217 against Vanderbilt) in a game. When he finished his Alabama career, he ranked third all-time in receptions (102) and receiving yardage (1,611).

Alabama has never had a Heisman Trophy winner. As a junior for the Crimson Tide in 1993, David Palmer came the closest of any Bama player, finishing third. He was expected to be the 1994 favorite for the award given to the nation's finest football player, but Palmer decided to forego his senior season to enter the 1994 NFL Draft. He was a second-round draft choice of the Minnesota Vikings and played seven years of professional football.

fumble and the Buffaloes got a final-play field goal for a 12–10 halftime lead.

Palmer seemed to have given Bama a go-ahead score early in the third quarter. Playing quarterback, he scooted in from eight yards out, but Alabama committed an illegal substitution on the play. Bama saved the series when Barker passed to Siran Stacy, who lunged into the end zone. In the back-and-forth game, Alabama took the lead for good late in the third quarter when Barker connected with Kevin Lee for a touchdown.

Palmer was winner of the Brian Piccolo Trophy, given to the Most Valuable Player in the game. He had two kickoff returns for 37 yards, five punt returns for 72 yards, six rushes for 21 yards, and two receptions for 14 yards.

Following the game, Stallings said, "That David Palmer is something. He's done that kind of thing all year when we've needed it. I'm sure glad he's playing for us. When the Good Lord was passing out ability, he spent some time at that youngster's house."

Alabama safety Stacy Harrison, whose sack forced the Colorado punt that Palmer returned for a touchdown, was asked about Palmer. "Heisman," he said. "That's all I've got to say. Heisman."

Game Details

Alabama 30 • Colorado 25

Alabama	7	3	13	7	30
Colorado	7	5	7	6	25

Date: December 28, 1991

Team Records: Alabama 10–1, Colorado 8–2–1

Scoring Plays:

UA Palmer 52-yard punt return (Wethington kick)

CU Phillips 1-yard rush (Harper kick)

CU Safety (Houston tackled by T. Johnson)

UA Wethington 25-yard field goal

CU Harper 33-yard field goal

UA Stacy 13-yard pass from Barker (run failed)

CU Westbrook 62-yard pass from Hagan (Harper kick)

UA Lee 12-yard pass from Barker (Wethington kick)

UA Palmer 5-yard pass from Barker (Wethington kick)

CU C. Johnson 13-yard pass from Hagan (pass failed)

Alabama's coaching staff is better than the average college coaching staff. I'd say it's a full notch better.

—BILL McCARTNEY, COLORADO HEAD COACH

Unforgettable
Moments

September 22, 1962

Meet Mr. Namath

Joe Willie Namath Bombs Georgia in Inaugural Outing

Alabama's first four seasons under Paul Bryant were composed of those Southern football staples—defense and kicking. When Joe Namath was added to the mix in 1962, it was as surprising as if the Dreamland Bar-B-Q menu had added pâté de foie gras.

Bama had been winning, to be sure. With Pat Trammell at quarterback, the Crimson Tide had gone undefeated and won the 1961 national championship. There were a few blowouts in those early seasons, but far more games were won with just a few points for Alabama and zero or thereabouts for opponents.

Namath won the Alabama starting quarterback job over Jack Hurlbut with a sensational performance in the final scrimmage before the season-opening game against Georgia. Reports from Tuscaloosa practice had it that Namath had completed all seven of his pass attempts for 81 yards and had also run for a touchdown.

Crimson Tide fans couldn't wait to see the sophomore from Beaver Falls, Pennsylvania. Namath already had a reputation, though not the "Broadway Joe" persona he would earn in the future. Namath had originally signed with Maryland, but wasn't able to get into school there. He had been directed to Alabama.

The first time Alabama players saw him was when he came onto the practice field in August 1961. "He was wearing a zoot suit and a little porkpie hat," tight end Tommy Brooker said. "Coach Bryant had him come up on the tower with him. We had never seen anyone but Coach Bryant on the tower." Bryant coached from a tower, 30 feet above the practice fields, so he could survey all. As many players can attest, when necessary he would come down from his perch to give individual lessons.

In late September, Namath was wearing crimson jersey No. 12. He would start his first game at quarterback in the season opener. Namath said that prior to the game, "I had a headache, a terrible headache, one of those throbbing headaches. We went out on the field, the band started playing, and my headache disappeared."

Namath's first play at quarterback didn't excite anyone. "I called a quarterback sneak behind Lee Roy Jordan," Namath said. "I just wanted to get hit to settle down. We didn't make a first down and punted."

Joe Namath made an instant impact upon taking over at quarterback for Alabama, throwing three touchdowns in his debut against Georgia.
Photo courtesy of AP Images

"On the first play after we got the ball back, Richard Williamson broke open on an 'out' pattern," Namath said. Williamson got behind the defender. The ball whistled into Williamson's hands at the Georgia 15, and the fleet receiver sprinted to the end zone. Joe Willie Namath's first Alabama pass was a 52-yard touchdown. Just 3:15 into the opening game, a new era in Alabama football had begun.

Namath finished 10-of-14 for 179 yards and three scores before being relieved in the fourth quarter by Hurlbut. Namath was named the National Back of the Week and Alabama was No. 1 in the polls.

"After the game in the dressing room, we were having a big time," Namath said. "The newspaper guys came in and started interviewing us. And I heard Coach Bryant say, 'Get away from the Popcorn Kid. Talk to the guys who did the winning.' Well, I took a little offense to Coach Bryant calling me a Popcorn Kid, and I must have showed it with my body language. I was standing next to Lee Roy and he kind of popped me with his forearm and said not to let it bother me. Coach Bryant had a way of keeping your head on straight."

Joe Namath

Joe Namath was an All-American at Alabama and is one of the most famous quarterbacks in football history. Even though injured much of his senior season, Namath came off the bench to complete 18 passes for 255 yards and a pair of touchdowns to earn the MVP award in the Tide's 1965 Orange Bowl loss to Texas. Despite the defeat, Alabama claimed the national championship. In his Alabama career he completed 203 of 374 passes for 2,714 yards and 25 touchdowns. Following the bowl game he became the most famous rookie in AFL history when he signed with the New York Jets for more than $400,000. He and Kenny Stabler were Alabama's quarterbacks on the Alabama Team of the Decade for the 1960s and for the Alabama Team of the Century. Namath went on to a Pro Football Hall of Fame career, highlighted by his guarantee that the upstart AFL Jets would beat the prohibitive favorite NFL Baltimore Colts of coach Don Shula in what would be Super Bowl III. Namath was MVP of that game as he delivered on his promise. The Jets' win is said to have been one of the most significant factors in the decision by the NFL to merge with the AFL. As "Broadway Joe," he was a cult figure, whose credits included memorable commercials and not-so-memorable movies. He earned his degree from Alabama in 2008.

> **A**labama still has the old master on defense. Alabama's defense was alert. It was always in the right place. You don't know what Bear Bryant's defense is until you try to coach an offense to score on him.
>
> —WALLY BUTTS, GEORGIA ATHLETICS DIRECTOR

Game Details

Alabama 35 • Georgia 0

Georgia	0	0	0	0	**0**
Alabama	9	6	6	14	**35**

Date: September 22, 1962

Team Records: Alabama 0–0, Georgia 0–0

Scoring Plays:

UA Williamson 52-yard pass from Namath (Davis kick)

UA Safety (Saye tackled in end zone)

UA Clark 10-yard pass from Namath (kick failed)

UA Clark 12-yard pass from Namath (run failed)

UA Clark 4-yard run (Wilson pass from Hurlbut)

UA Harris 25-yard run (run failed)

When Bryant met with the writers he said, "Namath did a beautiful job. Our passing was real good. The thing I liked best is we didn't have any interceptions."

Wally Butts spoke to the Tuscaloosa Quarterback Club on Monday after the game. Butts had retired as head football coach at Georgia following the 1960 season and was serving as athletics director for the Bulldogs. Butts got a roar of laughter when he said, "I think the Alabama team has a great future as soon as somebody teaches Joe Namath to throw the football."

Later, no one who had been involved in that Alabama-Georgia game would be laughing. The next spring the *Saturday Evening Post* published "The Story of a College Football Fix," based on the allegation that a Georgia insurance man had somehow been connected into a telephone conversation between Butts and Bryant, who was also Alabama's athletics director, a couple of weeks before the game. Convoluted notes purported to

Long before he became "Broadway Joe," Joe Namath led the Tide to a national championship in 1964.

prove Butts had given Bryant information to help Bama beat the Bulldogs.

"I was the quarterback and the quarterback called the plays," Namath said. "The coaches didn't call the plays."

Butts and Bryant filed suits against the publisher. Butts was awarded more than $3 million. Bryant settled for $320,000.

Bryant took the stand during the trial. An attorney for Curtis Publishing handed Bryant a note to read. Bryant patted his pocket and said, "I forgot my glasses." The attorney said he knew things were bad when every juror with glasses offered them to the coach.

Cornelius Bennett sacked quarterback Steve Beuerlein in the Tide's first victory over Notre Dame in school history. *Photo courtesy of Getty Images*

October 4, 1986

The Sack

Bennett's Crushing Tackle of Quarterback Propelled Tide over Notre Dame

Game-winning plays may seem to come most often from the offense or special teams and usually in the final moments of a football game, but it doesn't have to be that way. Alabama and Notre Dame were feeling one another out midway through the first quarter in 1986 when the game was decided. No points were scored, no turnover caused, not even field position changed. But the lights had been turned out on the Fighting Irish.

That was particularly true for Notre Dame quarterback Steve Beuerlein. The quarterback is the most important man on the field. He must think and see clearly. After the first quarter, however, Beuerlein was playing in a mental fog.

"I realized I was making some pretty stupid mistakes, like going the wrong way on plays," he said. "I remember seeing a lot of mouths moving, but I didn't hear the words that well."

Beuerlein had suffered a mild concussion at the hands of Alabama linebacker Cornelius Bennett.

Midway through the first quarter of a scoreless game, Bennett fired off the corner from the left side of the Alabama defense. Although Bennett did not come from Beuerlein's blind side, the Notre Dame quarterback admitted later he never saw Bennett coming. "I didn't see him," Beuerlein said. "I just felt him hit me, and I was on my back. I don't even remember if I had the ball or not."

Beuerlein didn't have the ball, but the official missed the fumble, ruling Beuerlein down for an eight-yard loss.

Beuerlein also didn't have control of his faculties. "I didn't say anything about it, but I probably should have taken myself out," Beuerlein said.

Bennett said, "I don't try to hurt anybody." He said no Notre Dame player took responsibility for blocking him. "Nobody picked me up. That's just something that happens every now and then. I put good pressure on him all day, but that was just one of the times that nobody picked me up. It's my job to get to the quarterback.

"Pass rushing is a lot of hard work. They seemed a little bit slow getting to me off the corner. That's

Cornelius Bennett was a dominating pass rusher and three-time All-American as a member of the Crimson Tide.

Cornelius Bennett

Cornelius Bennett was a three-time All-American, including being a unanimous selection his senior season of 1986. He won the Lombardi Award as the nation's top linebacker in 1986 and finished seventh in voting for the Heisman Trophy. Bennett was SEC Player of the Year as a senior. He was named Most Valuable Player in both the Aloha Bowl and Sun Bowl. Readers of 'BAMA Magazine selected him as Player of the Decade for the 1980s and he was named to the Alabama Team of the Century. He was inducted into the National Football Foundation Hall of Fame in 2003. Bennett was drafted second overall by Indianapolis in the 1987 NFL Draft. He played 14 years in the NFL (Buffalo, Atlanta, and Indianapolis) and played in five Super Bowls.

Anytime you go out, especially against a team like Notre Dame, and manhandle them like we did, you've got to enjoy it. I had a big smile the whole day, because I really did have some fun today.

—CORNELIUS BENNETT,
ALABAMA LINEBACKER

why I came off the corner full speed the whole game. It seemed they couldn't stop me. Anytime it's like that, look out."

"Their pass rush caused us a lot of problems," Notre Dame guard Shawn Heffern said. "Bennett has to be one of the best players I've ever played against. But he's not only a good football player, he's a class guy. We saw him on films and we knew he was good. He's certainly as good as they say."

Notre Dame coach Lou Holtz was also impressed with the Alabama pass rush. "They can put tremendous pressure on you," he said. "At least on us, they had a tremendous outside rush. They had three sacks. They forced us into a lot of turnovers. We threw three interceptions. It starts with the pass rush they were able to generate."

The pass rush affected the Notre Dame strategy. Beuerlein said, "We knew there were weaknesses in the Tide secondary, but we didn't have the time to get it done. They wouldn't let us do that, and it took our game plan away. We were too worried about what was going on up front. Defensively, they are the toughest we've played because of the speed factor. They make things happen so fast."

Beuerlein said that was true particularly of Bennett. "It was to the point that I was trying to figure out where he was before the snap and realize where he was going to be coming from," Beuerlein said. "That's something you really don't want to be thinking about before the play even gets started.

"He's strong and quick and every bit the great player everyone said he was."

Beuerlein had an uncharacteristically poor day, completing just five of 16 passes for 66 yards with one interception. His backup, Terry Andrysiak, also threw an interception and went 8-of-18 for 90 yards.

"Bennett is a great player," Andrysiak said. "He puts the pressure on you and takes your mind off what you're supposed to be doing. It was the toughest defense we've faced. And their fans really got into the game."

Game Details

Alabama 28 • Notre Dame 10

Notre Dame	0	10	0	0	**10**
Alabama	7	14	7	0	**28**

Date: October 4, 1986
Team Records: Alabama 4–0, Notre Dame 1–2
Scoring Plays:
UA Richardson 66-yard punt return (Tiffin kick)
UA Bell 52-yard pass from Shula (Tiffin kick)
ND Brown 8-yard pass from Beuerlein (Carney kick)
UA Cross 11-yard pass from Shula (Tiffin kick)
ND Carney 22-yard field goal
UA Bell 22-yard pass from Shula (Tiffin kick)

Alabama held Notre Dame after the sack of Beuerlein, and momentum swung to Alabama. The Irish punted to Greg Richardson who returned the kick 66 yards for a touchdown. The Tide never trailed.

It was Alabama's first win over Notre Dame. The Irish had taken a one-point win and the national championship in the 1973 Sugar Bowl, had denied Bama a national championship in 1974 with a two-point win in the 1975 Orange Bowl, and had two regular-season wins over Bama. Under his jersey and shoulder pads, Alabama quarterback Mike Shula wore a T-shirt with the inscription, "The Luck Stop Here."

> **I** really pay a special tribute to a fine, fine Alabama team. They came prepared to play. The better football team won today. It was no fluke.
> —LOU HOLTZ, NOTRE DAME COACH

November 9, 1996

Alexander the Great

Shaun Alexander Made the Most of His Chance at LSU

Dennis Riddle had rushed for a career-high 184 yards against Tennessee in Alabama's previous game. In the first half at Baton Rouge, however, Riddle fumbled. Crimson Tide coach Gene Stallings was not one to hide his feelings, and the coach obviously was upset with Riddle over the miscue.

Backup tailback Curtis Alexander had a wrap on his wrist as he continued to recover from injury. So Alabama turned to its third-team tailback, redshirt freshman Shaun Alexander. Alexander picked up 17 yards and a touchdown on his only carry of the first half. Bama had a 7–0 lead and Stallings had plans to let Alexander have a few more opportunities in the second half.

But Riddle was still at the top of the depth chart. He finished out the first half and started the second half. Midway through the third quarter, Stallings gave Alexander another chance.

Alexander took advantage.

In the third quarter Alexander would break two long touchdown runs behind the blocking of left tackle Chris Samuels, left guard Will Friend, and center John Causey. Tight end Patrick Hape was in the slot. Hape and fullback Trevis Smith (getting his first start because of an injury to Ed Scissum) were lead blockers. Michael Vaughn was at flanker.

Alexander took the handoff from quarterback Freddie Kitchens at the Alabama 27 and burst through the hole created by his blockers. He pulled out of one tackle, then got a final brush block from Malone and cruised into the end zone. The 73-yard run was the longest of any Bama running back that season.

Redshirt freshman tailback Shaun Alexander set an Alabama record with 291 yards rushing against LSU in 1996.

Shaun Alexander

Shaun Alexander was the Southeastern Conference Player of the Year as a senior in 1999. He was a two-time All-SEC performer and second-team All-American. He was a finalist for the Doak Walker Award as the best back in America and was Academic All-SEC. Alexander led the SEC in rushing as a senior. He became just the second Alabama running back to amass more than 3,000 yards rushing in a career with 3,565. Alexander set three SEC records and 15 Alabama records. He had 15 career 100-yard rushing performances and three 200-yard games, including the all-time Alabama record 291 yards against LSU. For his career he had 4,553 yards (3,565 rushing, 798 receiving, 90 kickoff return). He scored 302 points, the most in Bama history by a non-kicker. He was a three-time All-Pro performer and 2005 NFL MVP after being drafted in the first round by Seattle in 2000. He also played for the Washington Redskins.

Shaun Alexander is one of only three Alabama running backs to amass more than 3,000 rushing yards during their college careers.

Eight minutes later, Bama went back to the well, handing off to Alexander over left tackle. In the waning seconds of the third quarter, Alexander tacked on the second-longest run an Alabama back had in 1996. He went 72 yards, one yard shorter than the earlier run. Malone didn't get downfield in time to help with blocking, but he did stop and pay homage to Alexander with a royal bow, hands outstretched.

Although the big plays were Alexander's two long touchdowns at left end, he also proved he could go to his right. In the fourth quarter Alexander scored his fourth touchdown on a 12-yard run around right end. With three minutes to play in the game, Alexander made his last carry, another run around right end for 12 yards. The second carry wasn't a touchdown, but it did give him 291 yards rushing, breaking the Alabama record of 284 yards held by Bobby Humphrey. Alexander's four touchdowns tied a Bama record held by a handful of Tiders, including Riddle earlier in the year against Kentucky.

Alexander had rushed 19 times for 274 yards in the second half. Prior to the game at LSU, Alexander had carried a total of only 28 times for 144 yards and one touchdown. His two long runs at left end against the Bengal Tigers were for 145 yards, bettering his previous season total. Alexander averaged 14.6 yards per carry and Alabama averaged six yards per snap.

Alabama held LSU to 52 yards rushing, only 45 by outstanding back Kevin Faulk. "Alabama's defense lived up to its statistics," Faulk said. "They didn't do anything different than they usually do: great front seven and a great secondary. Alabama just has a great defense."

Alabama had not lost a game to LSU in Baton Rouge since 1969, going 13–0–1 in that streak.

Following the game, Stallings asked reporters how many yards Alexander had rushed for. Told the final total was 291, Stallings smiled and said, "Not too bad." Stallings complimented Alexander's size, speed, and ability to see the field, but also gave credit to the offensive line.

Alexander was on cloud nine. "I dreamed about this," he said. "I always want to play a lot. I think this game

> **T**here have been a lot of great backs at Alabama and Shaun is only a freshman and breaks the all-time record for rushing in a game. I'd say he's one of those great Alabama backs, too.
>
> —FREDDIE KITCHENS, ALABAMA QUARTERBACK

Game Details

Alabama 26 • LSU 0

Alabama	0	7	12	7	**26**
LSU	0	0	0	0	**0**

Date: November 9, 1996
Team Records: Alabama 7–1, LSU 6–1
Scoring Plays:

UA Alexander 17-yard rush (Brock kick)
UA Alexander 73-yard rush (kick failed)
UA Alexander 72-yard rush (pass failed)
UA Alexander 12-yard rush (Brock kick)

shows I can play at this level. I want to play and get better. The key is to keep on getting better in practice."

Stallings was asked if Alexander had earned starting status on the basis of his record-breaking game. "Not yet," Stallings said. "We knew for a long time that Shaun was going to be a good player. Still, there's more to football than running the ball."

The next week, Alexander was back to third team, behind Dennis Riddle and Curtis Alexander. He didn't get his first start until the opening game of his junior season in 1998.

Alabama rode a dominant second half by Derrick Thomas to an 8–3 victory over Penn State in 1988.

October 22, 1988

Lions Tamer

Derrick Thomas' Sack for Safety Highlighted His Game of Games

Alabama linebacker George Bethune had an injured neck and didn't get to play against Penn State. He stood on the sideline and watched his roommate and fellow linebacker, Derrick Thomas. "I guess I'll hear about this for a week," Bethune could joke later. The performance by Thomas was worth talking about.

Thomas—"the Sackman," as he came to be known—had been fantastic in an Alabama victory over the Nittany Lions of coach Joe Paterno.

"Derrick Thomas played perhaps his finest game," said Alabama coach Bill Curry. "We made some changes to free up Derrick. Once Derrick gets to flying around, all sorts of things happen. They start looking for him and try to compensate. It's a real nightmare for an offense when there's a player like that on the other team."

Thomas didn't start out as the dominating player in a defensive struggle. Alabama and

Penn State were tied 3–3 at halftime and Thomas had not made a tackle.

Alabama's defense under coordinator Don Lindsey was unconventional. (An opposing head coach said Alabama was hard to prepare for because "you can't know what they are going to do, and I'm not sure they know.") Thomas was known as the "strike," which ordinarily played as a strong-side linebacker.

Lindsey said, "I told Derrick before the game that we might make an adjustment with him sometime during the game. I wasn't going to tell the other guys. It was a monumental adjustment for him, and I didn't want any of the others thinking about it. We were just going to bring him from different places—the wide side, the middle, to the formation, away from the formation. In my mind, I had a plan on what to call."

Thomas had drawn double teams through most of the first half. In the second half, Lindsey explained, defensive tackle Thomas Rayam was moved to an end position.

Derrick Thomas

Derrick Thomas was a unanimous All-American in 1988 and winner of the Butkus Award as the nation's top college linebacker. Both CBS and the Washington Pigskin Club named him Defensive Player of the Year. He was selected the Alabama Defensive Player of the Decade by readers of *'BAMA Magazine* and an honoree on the Alabama Team of the Century. He set the school record for sacks with 18 in 1987 and broke that record with 27 in 1988. He was 10th in Heisman Trophy balloting. Thomas was the fourth player chosen in the 1989 NFL Draft and was NFL Rookie of the Year for the Kansas City Chiefs. He played 11 years for Kansas City and was selected to nine Pro Bowls. He had 126.5 career sacks, including an NFL-record seven in one game. He also set Chiefs records for safeties, forced fumbles, and fumble recoveries. He was 1993 NFL Man of the Year. He died in 2000 from complications following an automobile accident; in 2009 he was posthumously inducted into the Pro Football Hall of Fame.

Derrick Thomas played the game of his life today, and that's saying a lot.
—BILL CURRY, ALABAMA COACH

Derrick Thomas won the Butkus Award as the nation's top linebacker in 1988; his life was tragically cut short after an automobile accident in 2000.

Alabama's normal defense was a four-man line. Thomas became the fifth man on the line. As the Bama defensive huddle broke, Thomas would look to the sideline for a hand signal from Lindsey—left, right, or middle.

The idea, Lindsey said, was to make it more difficult for Penn State to locate Thomas. "The key was to get more pressure on the quarterback," Lindsey said.

Thomas said, "Coach Lindsey was saying, 'We're not going to sit back and let them dictate what we're going to do.' I was very pleased when he decided to go with the scheme."

Tony Sacca was the first freshman to be a starting quarterback at Penn State. During one fourth-quarter sequence, Thomas broke up a Sacca pass, sacked Sacca for a nine-yard loss, and caused a delay-of-game penalty as Sacca watched Thomas move from one rush position to another.

However, Lindsey said Bama's plan wasn't because Sacca was a freshman, but rather a tribute to Sacca's ability. "We would have done it if the Miami Dolphins' quarterback had been back there," Lindsey said. "We blitzed out of respect. We knew if we didn't put heat on him he would sit back in the pocket and throw a lot of completions."

Game Details

Alabama 8 • Penn State 3

Penn State	0	3	0	0	**3**
Alabama	0	3	3	2	**8**

Date: October 22, 1988

Team Records: Alabama 4–1, Penn State 4–2

Scoring Plays:
UA Doyle 39-yard field goal
PSU Tarasi 36-yard field goal
UA Doyle 35-yard field goal
UA Safety (Sacca tackled by Thomas)

Alabama's defense played very well against Penn State, but the Lions were containing Bama's offense, too. The Crimson Tide had gotten good running from Murry Hill, who would finish with 25 carries for 137 yards, and good passing from walk-on quarterback David Smith, who completed 18 of 38 passes for 186 yards. But no Tider could make it to the end zone. In the third quarter, Philip Doyle got his second field goal for a 6–3 Bama lead, but that was an uneasy advantage.

Chris Mohr had an excellent day punting, and his early fourth-quarter punt put Penn State at its 13-yard line. A penalty put the Lions on their 8. Sacca wanted to pass out of the end zone. He never had a chance.

Thomas was on the right side and went in almost untouched.

"I was there just as he started to set up," Thomas said. "I didn't realize it was a safety until I looked down on the ground and realized there were no hash marks. We were in the end zone."

It was one of three sacks of Sacca by Thomas in the second half. Thomas also had eight solo tackles, two of them behind the line of scrimmage. He batted down three passes.

Paterno said, "Our field position was horrendous in the second half. The first half, they didn't play us as aggressively. We figured they would start to come after us more in the second half."

When safety Lee Ozmint intercepted Penn State's last-gasp pass with 20 seconds to play, Bama could breathe easy. Everyone but Derrick Thomas, that is. Thomas had a difficult time breathing because a slight rib injury made inhaling painful. "I just had to sit and rest and get some oxygen," he said.

November 20, 1999

Sack for a Safety

Kindal Moorehead Ignited Tide for First Win at Jordan-Hare Stadium

Frequently a safety is worth more than the two points awarded. The team losing the two points also must kick (either a punt or place-kick) from its 20-yard line, often resulting in very good field position for the receiving team. That good field position can translate into even more points.

Moreover, a safety can be demoralizing for the victim, uplifting for the opponent.

Such was the case on Alabama's fifth trip to Jordan-Hare Stadium. The Crimson Tide had lost in its four previous excursions to Auburn, including some frustrating losses that should have been victories.

The Alabama team under head coach Mike DuBose was fundamentally unusual. Auburn opponents had been successful running the ball, but the Tide had a different tack. Bama came out throwing and had little success. Auburn had taken a 14–6 halftime lead as Tigers quarterback Ben Leard completed two touchdown passes in the second quarter. Although the Tide changed quarterbacks

from Andrew Zow to Tyler Watts for the second half, the biggest change was in strategy. It was almost too late.

Early in the third quarter, Alabama dodged a bullet as Auburn missed a 22-yard field goal. The Tide offense drove deep into Tigers territory, but couldn't score on three runs from the 2-yard line. That gave Auburn a big boost in momentum, but bad field position. Alabama star halfback Shaun Alexander was the man stopped on the fourth-down play. When he got to the sideline, DuBose told him, "God has blessed you with a lot of talent. You are capable of taking the game over."

But the first order of business was to get the football back. That would come in just one play.

Rather than dig out of the hole and protect their eight-point lead, Leard was called on to pass from the end zone.

To this day there is discussion over which Alabama player should have been credited for the sack. Middle linebacker Saleem Rasheed came from Leard's left, but was effectively held and couldn't make the play. Rasheed did, however, have Leard's attention.

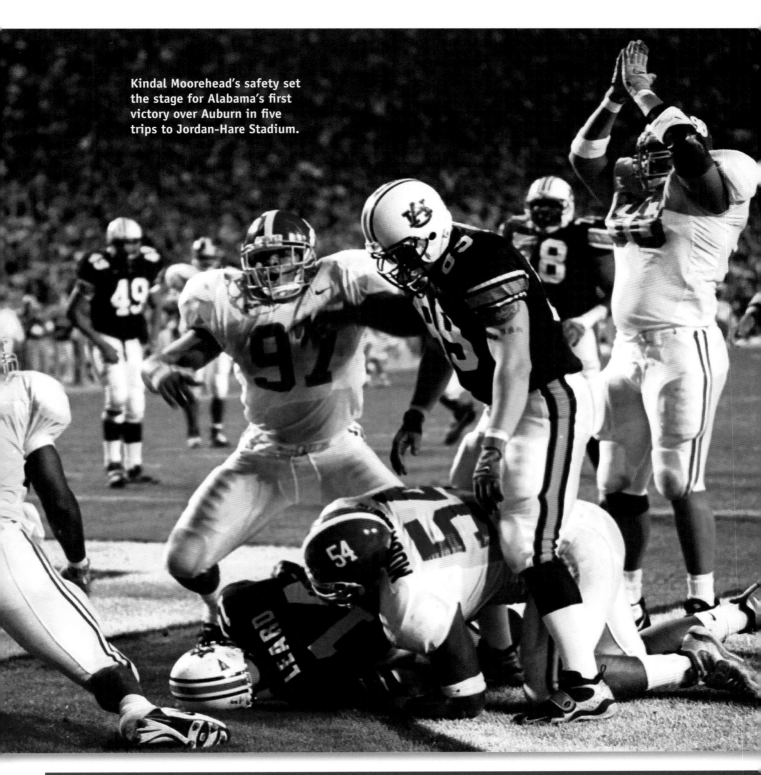

Kindal Moorehead's safety set the stage for Alabama's first victory over Auburn in five trips to Jordan-Hare Stadium.

Alabama vs. Auburn

The Alabama-Auburn series is considered to be the most bitter college football rivalry in the nation. It pits the state university, Alabama, which has long been one of the nation's traditional college football powers, against the land-grant university, Auburn.

The teams played against one another for the first time in 1893; Auburn won 32–22 at Lakeview Park in Birmingham. In 2008—some 115 years later—the teams had played only 73 times. That's because after a dispute over finances for the game, the teams broke off football relations from 1907 until 1948, even though the teams were in the same conferences. Under the threat of legislative action to force the game to be played annually, the leaders of the two colleges arranged the renewal of the series. For many years the game was played at Legion Field in Birmingham, but since 1989 Auburn has played its home games in Auburn and since 2000 Bama has played its home games in Tuscaloosa. Alabama has a commanding lead in games won over all its SEC opponents, including Auburn.

Shaun Alexander followed Kindal Moorehead's safety with an eight-yard touchdown run to give Alabama the Iron Bowl victory.

> **I** tell both quarterbacks the same thing. I tell both of them, "Give me the ball."
> —SHAUN ALEXANDER,
> ALABAMA TAILBACK

Meanwhile, tackle Cornelius Griffin was coming up the middle. Even though he went down for a moment, he was quickly back up and charging. And from Leard's right came end Kindal Moorehead.

The crash in the end zone was emphatic, Leard and his blockers collapsing together under the push of Rasheed, Griffin, and Moorehead. Perhaps because he delivered an unobstructed tackle, Moorehead was given credit for the sack in the end zone, and Alabama was awarded two points for the safety.

The comeback, which would become a runaway, had begun.

Moorehead said Auburn changed the play at the line. "They had the tight end on me, and I knew I could beat him. He was holding me, but I threw him to the outside and got to the quarterback," he said.

Griffin was a little surprised to see Leard drop straight back. He said, "I got cut, but got back on my feet and went after him. We got to him and dropped him for the safety."

Leard said, "I couldn't really see. I didn't want to throw it into the air. I decided to give away two points instead of throwing an interception and giving away more."

Freddie Milons, best known as Alabama's record-setting pass receiver, was a versatile player. He returned the kick following the safety to midfield. On a fourth-and-3 at the Auburn 16, Milons and Alexander lined up next to one another in the backfield and Milons took a direct snap from center. Milons picked up eight yards on the carry. On the next play, Alexander took it eight yards to the end zone. Bama had taken a 15–14 fourth-quarter lead and would not trail again.

Bama's defense held, Milons had a good punt return, and Alexander got his second touchdown of the fourth quarter.

Auburn closed to within 22–17 on a field goal and tried an onside kick. Alabama got the ball and planned to run out the clock, but Alexander ran it into the end zone, his third touchdown run in the fourth quarter.

Alexander had an explanation for his second-half explosion. In the first half he lost a contact lens. "I wasn't

Game Details

Alabama 28 • Auburn 17

Alabama	6	0	2	20	**28**
Auburn	0	14	0	3	**17**

Date: November 20, 1999
Team Records: Alabama 8–2, Auburn 5–5
Scoring Plays:
UA Pflugner 33-yard field goal
UA Pflugner 41-yard field goal
AU Diamond 7-yard pass from Leard (Duval kick)
AU Cooper 15-yard pass from Leard (Duval kick)
UA Safety (Leard tackled by Moorehead)
UA Alexander 8-yard rush (Pflugner kick)
UA Alexander 5-yard rush (Pflugner kick)
AU Duval 35-yard field goal
UA Alexander 6-yard rush (kick failed)

seeing the hole," he said. "I learned a lesson. When something like that happens, I need to come out because I'm hurting the team. I also learned that I'm really blind without my contacts."

It was a record-setting day for Alexander, who became Bama's all-time career rushing leader and passed Georgia's Herschel Walker for the SEC record for rushing touchdowns in a season; and for Milons, who became the Crimson Tide's single-season receptions leader. Moorehead, the sophomore left end who started the comeback, had two sacks on the day. Auburn's Leard had not suffered an interception all season. On his final pass of the game, Bama's Reggie Myles picked it off.

Alabama went from the win over Auburn to a romp over Florida in the SEC Championship Game before closing out the season with an overtime loss to Michigan in the Orange Bowl—Bama's 50th bowl game appearance.

December 31, 1975

Good Times in New Orleans

Ozzie Newsome's Catch Ignites Bama in Sugar Bowl

Alabama had arrived for the Sugar Bowl contest with Penn State a week before the game, and there was no curfew for Crimson Tide players the first two nights. On the third night, about two dozen players, many of them starters, decided to ignore the curfew. Bad idea. There was a bed check that night.

At breakfast the next morning, the curfew violators got to meet with Alabama coach Paul Bryant.

Crimson Tide quarterback Richard Todd was one of those at the breakfast lecture. "Coach Bryant said if it had just been one or two of us that he'd just send us home and kick us off the team," Todd said. "But since there were so many, he didn't feel he could kick everyone off and gut the team just before the bowl game. He said, 'What I'm going to do is send your name and the time you were out to your hometown newspaper. So this year if we lose the bowl game, they won't blame me.'

"And he did it. He sent the names of everyone who was late to their hometown newspapers. And it was in all the newspapers. You think about him being a disciplinarian, and he was. What he did was not cripple the team, which wouldn't have been fair to the innocent players, but he

made us accept responsibility for what we had done. I think that helped us win the game. We didn't want to be blamed for losing."

Alabama had not won a bowl game since the 1966 team had rolled over Nebraska in the Sugar Bowl to complete an 11–0 season. There had been seven losses and a tie since then.

The 1975 Alabama team had lost its opening game to Missouri 20–7, but won the next 10 games and went to New Orleans as the No. 3 team in the nation. The Penn State team of Joe Paterno would provide the opposition in the first Sugar Bowl game to be played in the new Louisiana Superdome.

A handful of those missing curfew in New Orleans were second-time offenders and were held out of the starting lineup. But the substitutes were pretty good. Ozzie Newsome, ordinarily the starting wide receiver, moved to tight end; Woodrow Lowe got a start at linebacker; and Mark Prudhomme became the starter at safety.

The move of Newsome to tight end resulted in Joe Dale Harris getting the start at wide receiver. Early in the game Todd connected with Harris on a 54-yard gain to the Penn State 20-yard line, resulting in Bama getting a 3–0 lead on a Danny Ridgeway field goal.

Ozzie Newsome caught a long fourth-quarter pass to set up the winning touchdown against Penn State in the 1975 Sugar Bowl.

Richard Todd

Richard Todd was the quarterback on the 1975 All–Southeastern Conference team and captain of the 1975 Crimson Tide. He split time with Gary Rutledge as a sophomore and took over starting duties for his junior and senior seasons. In addition to being a productive passer, he was a top rusher for Bama. He completed 10 of 12 passes for 210 yards and was awarded the Miller-Digby Trophy as the Most Valuable Player in the Sugar Bowl. He passed for 332 yards and two touchdowns in the Senior Bowl in his hometown of Mobile. He was the sixth player selected in the first round of the 1976 NFL Draft. His son, Gator, played on Alabama's golf team.

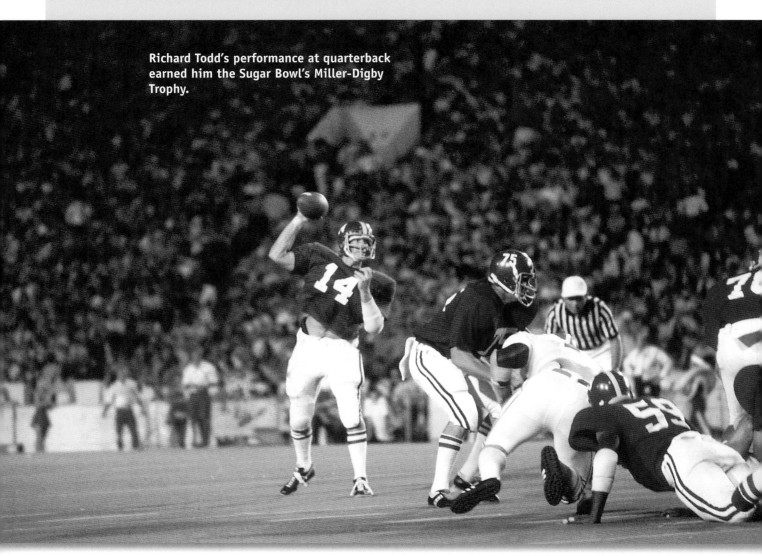

Richard Todd's performance at quarterback earned him the Sugar Bowl's Miller-Digby Trophy.

In the fourth quarter, with the game tied at 3–3, Alabama used its running game to move to a first down at the Crimson Tide 33-yard line. Another running play was the call, but when Todd got to the line of scrimmage, he didn't like what he saw.

Todd called timeout and went to the sideline. "Coach Bryant winked at me and called a long pass to Ozzie. He felt they'd be in single coverage on Ozzie. The coaches in the press box suggested something else. Coach Bryant told me to use my own judgment—the original running play, the long pass he suggested, or the play suggested from the assistant coaches," Todd said.

Todd went back and called the play suggested by Bryant—the long pass to Newsome, who had moved back to his normal position of split end. As Bryant knew, Penn State's starting cornerback had been injured earlier in the game, and Newsome was being covered by a 5'9" freshman.

Newsome began his route, cut sharply to the inside, then released straight downfield. Todd's pass was perfect, and the 6'2" Newsome took it to the Penn State 11-yard line. Two plays later, Mike Stock ran in behind a Newsome block for the game's only touchdown.

Alabama's 13–6 win over Penn State ended the streak of bowl games without a win. The Tide would go on to six consecutive bowl wins, including two that would win national championships for Alabama in the Louisiana Superdome.

Todd completed 10 of 12 passes for 210 yards, and Newsome caught four passes for 97 yards. Todd was a runaway winner of the Miller-Digby Award as the game's Most Valuable Player.

There had been some controversy before the game regarding Bryant's abundant influence in making bowl game matchups. Nebraska coach Tom Osborne wanted Alabama to play the winner of the Oklahoma-Nebraska game in the Orange Bowl. Osborne suggested Alabama was ducking Nebraska and Oklahoma to play a weaker team in Penn State. Nebraska lost to Arizona in the Fiesta Bowl while Oklahoma defeated Michigan in the Orange Bowl to win the national championship.

Following the game, Joe Paterno and Todd had a chance to shake hands on the field. Todd told the Penn State coach that Todd's plans included playing in the Senior Bowl. Paterno said, "I'd like to recommend you for that one. It's the least I can do since Coach Bryant recommended me for this one."

Game Details

Alabama 13 • Penn State 6

Alabama	3	0	7	3	**13**
Penn State	0	0	3	3	**6**

Date: December 31, 1975
Team Records: Alabama 10–1, Penn State 9–2
Scoring Plays:
UA Ridgeway 25-yard field goal
PSU Bahr 42-yard field goal
UA Stock 14-yard rush (Ridgeway kick)
PSU Bahr 37-yard field goal
UA Ridgeway 28-yard field goal

The thing that sets Alabama apart from [wishbone] teams like Texas A&M or Oklahoma is the passing of Richard Todd. Once they get you thinking run, he can step back and throw the ball extremely well. Some wishbone teams have to live and die with their running games. Not this team.

—JOE PATERNO, PENN STATE COACH

November 17, 2001

Opening the Floodgates

Zow's Pass to McAddley Set Stage for Rout in Auburn

There are recruiting mistakes, and there are *big* recruiting mistakes. In 1996, Alabama and Auburn were recruiting Andrew Zow, an outstanding athlete from Lake Butler, Florida. Zow committed to Auburn, which was recruiting him as a linebacker. Alabama assistant coach Jeff Rouzie asked Zow to reconsider, telling the youngster Alabama needed a quarterback.

Quarterback?

"I didn't take my commitment to Auburn lightly," Zow said. "I had given my word." But after consultation with his family, Zow decided he wanted to be a quarterback, as he had been in high school. Auburn came back with a matching quarterback offer, but it was too late. Andrew Zow was headed to Tuscaloosa.

Auburn didn't expect to see much of Zow when Alabama went to Auburn in 2001. The Tigers were preparing for Tyler Watts to quarterback the Crimson Tide. Watts was an option quarterback, while Zow was strictly a drop-back passer.

Zow had been Bama's starter from the last few games of his freshman year in 1998 through the first half of his junior year, but had played very little as a senior. He had,

however, been in Auburn before. Zow quarterbacked the Tide's SEC championship team to a 28–17 victory in 1999. But in 2001, Zow would play only 33 snaps in the first eight games. When Watts was injured against Mississippi State, Zow came in and led the Tide to victory.

Auburn knew that Watts was injured but still expected him to start the game. "He's from this state," Auburn coach Tommy Tuberville said. "How can he not play in this game? It's just a groin pull. Some of our guys are playing with those."

Zow, a senior, said, "I didn't tell anyone who was starting. I wanted them to prepare for two quarterbacks. Tyler runs the option better than anybody we've had. With me we do a little more throwing. We knew how to attack them. We may not run the same plays with me in the game that we would with Tyler in the game, but our offense is not the same every week anyway."

Auburn defensive coordinator John Lovett was among those who confessed to a miscalculation. "We spent a lot of time working on the option, which we didn't see," he said.

Although the final score was a convincing 31–7 in Bama's favor, the game was close until just before halftime.

Jason McAddley's touchdown just before halftime gave the Tide momentum en route to a 31–7 thrashing of Auburn.

Andrew Zow

After a redshirt season in 1997, Andrew Zow took over the starting quarterback job in the fifth game of his first year of play for Alabama. He was an 11-game starter in 1999, leading the Crimson Tide to an overtime win over Florida in Gainesville. Zow split time with Tyler Watts as Bama beat the Gators again in the SEC Championship Game. He and Watts also split playing time in 2000 with Zow starting seven games. His senior year could have been a great disappointment as he played only 33 snaps through the first eight games. When Watts suffered a pulled groin, Zow came on to lead a comeback win over Mississippi State, a rout of Auburn, a win over Southern Miss in the game postponed because of 9/11, and a win over Iowa State in the Independence Bowl. When he finished his Alabama career, he had set Alabama passing records with 459 completions, 852 attempts, and 5,983 yards, and had tied Mike Shula for touchdown passes at 35. He was Academic All-SEC and team captain as a senior.

Originally committed to Auburn, Andrew Zow changed his mind and enrolled at Alabama after being offered a chance to play quarterback.

Both teams missed field goals in the scoreless first quarter, but Auburn was the big loser in that opening stanza. Tigers star running back, freshman Carnell "Cadillac" Williams, had run on five of the first six plays of the game and gained 39 yards, including 24 on a busted play. But on the sixth play he was lost with a broken collarbone.

Alabama drew first blood with a nice drive that ended in an eight-yard run for a touchdown by tailback Santonio Beard. Auburn matched it with a short drive after a good kickoff return.

As halftime approached, it appeared the game would be tied at intermission. Alabama had the ball but was struggling with its drive. Bama had moved into Auburn territory with about a minute to play. Zow went back to pass and found himself surrounded by Tigers intent on a sack. Zow leaned to his right and with a sidearm motion zipped a pass downfield. Crimson Tide split end Jason McAddley had gotten behind the Auburn secondary.

McAddley said, "I saw Andrew scrambling back there, and I saw that somebody almost had him around the ankles. I threw my arm up, and he threw a good ball, even though he was just about to fall down. He hit me right on the money. It was a big play, because it gave us momentum right before halftime."

Alabama had gone up 14–7. Moreover, because Auburn had won the game-opening toss and elected to receive, Bama would get the ball to start the second half. That would prove pivotal.

Following the second-half kickoff, Alabama used just two plays to go 80 yards and make it 21–7. The drive had taken only 21 seconds. Zow completed a pass of 33 yards to Freddie Milons on first down, and Beard ran 47 yards to the end zone on the next play.

"It had to be deflating," Tide coach Dennis Franchione said. "A few seconds before halftime it looks like it's going to be 7–7, and then before Auburn can get its offense back on the field it's 21–7."

Zow completed 22 of 29 passes for 221 yards and two touchdowns, and emerged from the game as Alabama's career passing leader.

McAddley said, "Andrew has gone through a lot this year. He faced a lot of adversity, and he hasn't had a lot of opportunity for playing time, but he's a great team player. He never had a negative attitude. I think it hurt him to be a fifth-year senior and to not be the starting quarterback, but he's always been positive about his situation. He was able to come in and make some big, big plays.

"For him to go down to Auburn and break the passing record and help us win the game, I think it was one of the greatest games he ever played."

It was one of the all-time great games I've ever seen a quarterback play. I thanked him for playing the way he did. It made all of us feel so good.

—JOE NAMATH, FORMER ALABAMA QUARTERBACK

Game Details

Alabama 31 • Auburn 7

Alabama	0	14	7	10	**31**
Auburn	0	7	0	0	**7**

Date: November 17, 2001
Team Records: Alabama 4–5, Auburn 7–2
Scoring Plays:
UA Beard 8-yard rush (Thomas kick)
AU Brown 5-yard rush (Duval kick)
UA McAddley 45-yard pass from Zow (Thomas kick)
UA Beard 47-yard rush (Thomas kick)
UA Jones 10-yard pass from Zow (Thomas kick)
UA Thomas 26-yard field goal

Tide quarterback Jay Barker
outgunned Georgia's Eric Zeier to
lead Alabama over the Bulldogs
29–28 in 1994.

October 1, 1994

Good Night, Bulldogs

Barker and Malone Open Door for Bama Comeback

So much for "All he can do is win." That was the book on senior Alabama quarterback Jay Barker as the Crimson Tide prepared for a rare night game at Bryant-Denny Stadium in Tuscaloosa. He had a record of 27–1–1 as Alabama's quarterback, including being at the helm as a sophomore throughout the undefeated national championship season of 1992.

Nevertheless, Barker didn't get much credit. Coach Gene Stallings' plan for success was for the defense and kicking teams to make good plays, and for the offense to avoid bad plays.

When Georgia invaded, the contrast at quarterback was expected to be dramatic. Alabama had won its first four games, but Barker had been mediocre, with 37 completions in 63 attempts for 423 yards and only three touchdowns. On the Georgia side would be Heisman Trophy candidate Eric Zeier, who had completed 93 of 150 passes for 1,307 yards and nine touchdowns.

Georgia was determined to stop the Tide ground attack. That task was made easier by the fact that Bama's top rusher, Sherman Williams, was hampered with a sprained ankle. An offense has to take what it is given. Barker was happy to accept.

Bama would get fewer than 100 yards rushing against the Bulldogs, and Alabama hasn't often won a game with low rushing numbers. That lack of production on the ground, though, was more than offset by Barker and an unlikely target.

Alabama junior wide receiver Toderick Malone had been a solid, though less than spectacular, receiver. Going into 1994 he had a total of nine receptions. Through the first four games he ranked as Alabama's fourth receiver, pulling in just seven passes for 73 yards. He had a decent first half—three catches for 54 yards—but also had allowed two passes to escape through his hands. He would have a second half to remember.

Georgia had an outstanding secondary led by safety Will Muschamp, who years later became an excellent defensive coach at Auburn and Texas. The Alabama offense devised by offensive coordinator Homer Smith confused the Bulldogs.

Michael Proctor

Michael Proctor set an Alabama record in his first game as a freshman against Vanderbilt when he kicked four field goals. It was also a game in which he had an extra-point kick blocked, the only miss he would have in 132 PAT opportunities in his Crimson Tide career (1992–95). A two-time All-American, Proctor finished his career as Alabama's second leading scorer with 326 points. He was good on 65 of 91 field goals in his four years at Bama. He was All-SEC in 1993 and 1994 and was a 1993 finalist and 1994 semifinalist for the Lou Groza Award, given to the nation's best place-kicker. In 1992 he was a Freshman All-American. In 1993 against Southern Miss he had 15 points by kicking, second-best in Alabama history. His 97 kicking points in 1993 and 94 kicking points in 1992 rank third and fourth in Crimson Tide history. His mark of 131 career PATs ranks third. His 65 career field goals make him second in Alabama history.

Game Details:

Alabama 29 • Georgia 28

Georgia	7	14	7	0	**28**
Alabama	0	10	9	10	**29**

Date: October 1, 1994

Team Records: Alabama 4–0, Georgia 3–1

Scoring Plays:

UG Warner 9-yard pass from Zeier (Parkman kick)

UA Lynch 6-yard rush (Proctor kick)

UG Graham 23-yard pass from Zeier (Parkman kick)

UG Hunter 5-yard pass from Zeier (Parkman kick)

UA Proctor 33-yard field goal

UA Malone 35-yard pass from Barker (pass failed)

UA Proctor 35-yard field goal

UG Simpson 5-yard pass from Zeier (Parkman kick)

UA Malone 49-yard pass from Barker (Proctor kick)

UA Proctor 32-yard field goal

"We got our signals crossed," Muschamp said. "I'm the quarterback out there in the secondary, and it's my job to make sure everyone is lined up right. Any breakdown and it's my fault."

With the Tide trailing 21–10 in the second half, Barker and Malone went to work. Malone took a pass for 29 yards on the first play of the third quarter and caught an eight-yard pass on second down. A short run put the Tide at the Georgia 35.

Malone, lined up on the right side, gave an inside fake, then sprinted past Georgia defenders. He took Barker's pass in stride for a touchdown that cut the lead to 21–16.

But Zeier continued to make life miserable for Alabama's stop troops, and early in the fourth quarter the Bulldogs had expanded the lead to 28–19.

> **I** don't know how we lost. The Alabama defense put us in situations that were tough on us. We needed third-and-short, but seemed to always end up in third-and-long.
>
> —ERIC ZEIER, GEORGIA QUARTERBACK

Michael Proctor kicked the game-winning 32-yard field goal to cap Alabama's comeback.

Jay Barker

Jay Barker's legacy at Alabama is winning. No quarterback did better. In three years as a starter (1992–94), Barker quarterbacked Crimson Tide teams that went 34–2–1. He was on Alabama teams that won 45 games in four years. When he finished his college career, he held Alabama records for passing yards (5,699), completions (402), and attempts (706). Barker was quarterback of the undefeated 1992 national championship team that defeated previous No. 1 Miami and its Heisman Trophy quarterback, Gino Torretta. He was an All-American following his senior season and was presented with the Johnny Unitas Golden Arm Award, which goes to the nation's best quarterback based on academics, leadership, character,

> **Jay Barker had it in him. He's a tremendous player. He looked like [Joe] Montana in his prime.**
>
> **—HOMER SMITH,**
> **ALABAMA OFFENSIVE COORDINATOR**

and athletic achievement. He was a finalist for the Davey O'Brien Outstanding Quarterback Award and finished fifth in Heisman Trophy balloting. He was All–Southeastern Conference, Academic All–SEC, SEC Player of the Year, and team captain.

Barker opened the next drive with a Homer Smith special, a toss to fullback Tarrant Lynch that gained 23 yards. Then it was back to Malone. Again lined up on the right side, Malone gave the same fake and got the same result. He was behind the Georgia defensive backs and Barker took advantage, hitting him on a pass that would carry the remaining 49 yards. Score quickly? The "drive" took 42 seconds and pulled Alabama to within two points at 28–26.

Malone would finish the day with eight receptions for 173 yards, two of them on the inside-out route for 84 yards and two touchdowns.

It took a little more to get the victory.

Alabama had the ball at midfield with 2:10 to play after pinning Georgia deep in its own territory with a punt. Barker escaped from trouble and ran for 13 yards. Moments later he completed a pass to tight end Tony Johnson, who ran it down to the Georgia 16, a 22-yard gain. From there the Tide positioned the ball for Michael Proctor's game-winning 32-yard field goal.

Malone said, "We hung in there. I think our tradition had a lot to do with it. And Jay was throwing the ball exceptionally well."

Barker completed 26 of 34 passes for 396 yards, two touchdowns, and no interceptions. Zeier was as good as expected: 25-of-33 for 263 yards, four touchdowns, and one interception.

Barker spread the credit. He said, "I'm proud of the way that I played, but I'm even more proud of the offensive line, and the entire offense. There was a lot of confidence in our huddle."

Barker knew he had won a heavyweight fight. "It does raise the ante a little bit when a quarterback like Eric Zeier comes into town," Barker said. "Eric is the best quarterback I've ever been around."

Barker also remembered the game as the only one in which he was benched for poor play. "Coach Stallings said to just watch for a few minutes," he said. "It was exactly what I needed."

Acknowledgments

My name is on this book, but it was far from a one-person project.

The acknowledgments go deep, to my early writing mentors, Dean Stone at the *Maryville Times* in Tennessee and Bob Phillips at the *Birmingham Post-Herald*. I will be forever grateful to Charley Thornton, who brought me to Alabama as his assistant in what was known as the sports publicity office. As a part of my job, I talked football with Coach Bryant frequently, almost every day during football season for more than a dozen years. No value could be placed on that experience. There has been no one like him in my life.

During my time at Alabama and since founding *'BAMA Magazine* in 1979, I have had wonderful relationships with the coaches and players of the Crimson Tide, and I am grateful for the help I received from them in trying to be accurate and in putting these plays into context.

I owe much to the followers of Alabama athletics. The great interest in and support given to the Crimson Tide has allowed me to chronicle these stories. And, specific to this book, the website community on BamaMag.com provided significant and helpful input.

Cary L. Clark, a veteran sports reporter and longtime writer for *'BAMA Magazine*, provided excellent research assistance in both quality and quantity.

The Paul W. Bryant Museum—including director Ken Gaddy, Taylor Watson, Brad Green, and longtime Bryant assistant coach Clem Gryska—is a treasure, and I am indebted to the staff for its help and for many of the photographs in this book.

Kent Gidley, chief photographer for the Alabama athletics department, was a great help in securing photos. Stuart McNair is photographer for *'BAMA Magazine* and he, too, contributed.

Doug Layton, my good friend who has spent many decades behind a microphone, honored me by being kind enough to contribute the foreword.

I have a prejudice for the editor, having been one most of my adult life. I was fortunate enough to have an outstanding editor for this book. Linda McNair Cohen, my sister and formerly a librarian who helped many authors, put the polish on this work. But before she did that, she got out the spots. I cannot thank her enough for her conscientious attention.

This project could not have been done without the support of those closest to me—my family—and they have my deepest gratitude. My wife Lynne has known the long and inconvenient hours of sportswriting for more than 40 years. She has accepted our lot and shouldered much of the burden of our household. Our children, Julia and Stuart, had days and hours robbed, but managed to grow up well and are parents of perfect grandchildren.

Sources

Alabama Journal (1959–1971)

Anniston Star (1959–2008)

Atlanta Constitution (1959–2008)

Atlanta Journal (1959–2008)

'BAMA, Inside the Crimson Tide (1979–2009)

Birmingham News (1959–2008)

Birmingham Post-Herald (1959–2005)

Browning, Al. *Bowl Bama Bowl.* Huntsville, AL: Strode Publishers (1977)

Browning, Al. *Third Saturday in October.* Nashville, TN: Rutledge Hill Press (1987)

Crimson TIDE-Ings (1964–1978)

Crimson White (1964–1979)

Decatur Daily (1964–2008)

Forney, John. *Above the Noise of the Crowd.* Huntsville, AL: Albright & Company (1986)

Gadsden Times (1959–2008)

Huntsville Times (1959–2008)

McCollough, Dr. E. Gaylon. *The Long Shadow of Coach Paul "Bear" Bryant.* Gulf Shores, AL: Compass Press (2008)

McNair, Kirk. *What It Means to Be Crimson Tide.* Chicago: Triumph Books (2005)

Memphis Commerical Appeal (1959–2008)

Miami Herald (1959–2008)

Moble Press Register (1959–2008)

Montgomery Advertiser (1959–2008)

New Orleans Times-Picayune (1959–2008)

Southeastern Conference Football Media Guide (1970–2008)

Tuscaloosa News (1959–2008)

University of Alabama Football Media Guide (1964–2008)